Attitude

Your Most Priceless Possession

Fourth Edition

Elwood N. Chapman and Wil McKnight

A Crisp Fifty-Minute™ Series Book

This Fifty-Minute™ book is designed to be "read with a pencil." It is an excellent workbook for self-study as well as classroom learning. All material is copyright-protected and cannot be duplicated without permission from the publisher. *Therefore, be sure to order a copy for every training participant through our Web site, www.axzopress.com.*

Attitude

Your Most Priceless Possession

Fourth Edition

**Elwood N. Chapman and
Wil McKnight**

CREDITS:

VP, Product Development: **Adam Wilcox**
Production Editor: **Genevieve McDermott**
Manufacturing: **Julia Coffey**
Production Artists: **Nicole Phillips, Rich Lehl, and Betty Hopkins**
Cartoonist: **Ralph Mapson**

ISBN 10: 1-56052-664-5
ISBN 13: 978-1-56052-664-3
Library of Congress Catalog Card Number 2001095091
Printed in the United States of America

10 11 09 08

Learning Objectives For:

ATTITUDE

The objectives for *Attitude: Your Most Priceless Possession, Fourth Edition* are listed below. They have been developed to guide you the user the core issues covered in this book.

THE OBJECTIVES OF THIS BOOK ARE TO HELP THE USER:

1) Define attitude, to show its importance and effect on personality and work performance, and learn ways of keeping it positive

2) Explore specific techniques for retaining and recapturing a positive attitude

3) See the effect of a positive attitude on the work environment, especially its effect on workforce diversity, career success, and teamwork

4) Protect a positive attitude

5) Prepare an **Action Plan** that incorporates the ideas, concepts, and techniques presented in this book into your daily life

ASSESSING PROGRESS

A Crisp Series **assessment** is available for this book. The 25-item, multiple-choice and true/false questionnaire allows the reader to evaluate his or her comprehension of the subject matter.

To download the assessment and answer key, go to www.axzopress.com and search on the book title.

Assessments should not be used in any employee selection process.

About the Authors

The late Elwood N. Chapman retired in 1977 as a professor at Chaffey College and a visiting lecturer at Claremont Graduate School after 29 years of successful college teaching. He was a graduate of the University of California. Mr. Chapman was also co-founder of Crisp Publications, and author of more than a dozen books by Crisp.

Wil McKnight, author of this Fourth Edition, is a writer and third-generation publisher, primarily in the areas of supervisory training, vocational education, and work study.

Mr. McKnight has a B.A. from Carnegie Mellon University (back when they called it Carnegie Tech), and an M.B.A. from Stanford. He has written several self-study books and checklists for construction supervisors, some of them based on Crisp Publications. You can reach him via e-mail at wilmck3@aol.com.

In Memoriam

Elwood N. Chapman died in the fall of 1995. Known as "Chap" to his friends and colleagues, he touched the lives of many through his teaching and writing. Though Chap's typewriter is silent, he continues to speak to us through the books that remain his legacy. We miss his cheerful smile, twinkling eyes, and wonderful attitude.

Amoebas, hand-drawn by Chap, were a central theme in earlier editions of *Attitude*. Because they divide in two about every hour, they illustrate that the best way for humans to keep a positive attitude is to constantly renew it by sharing it with others. Amoebas also have no ethnicity, no age, and no gender, further symbolizing attitude as a characteristic enjoyed by all.

How to Use This Book

A Crisp Learning *Fifty-Minute*™ *Book* can be used in variety of ways. Individual self-study is one of the most common. However, many organizations use *Fifty-Minute* books for pre-study before a classroom training session. Other organizations use the books as a part of a system-wide learning program—supported by video and other media based on the content in the books. Still others work with Crisp Learning to customize the material to meet their specific needs and reflect their culture. Regardless of how it is used, we hope you will join the more than 20 million satisfied learners worldwide who have completed a *Fifty-Minute Book*.

Preface

Hardly anyone ever starts from scratch. In life—personal and at work—we all build on the results of those who've gone before: family, co-workers, people who earlier shaped the environments and situations that affect us today.

This fourth edition of *Attitude: Your Most Priceless Possession* builds on the foundation set by Elwood Chapman through three previous editions and his nearly fifty years of observation and reflection on questions like: "What is an attitude?" "Why are some people more positive than others?" "What can I do to stay positive?" "How can I restore my attitude when it sags?"

Changes in the fourth edition are subtle but important:

➤ It contains more examples, with additional details drawn from real situations.

➤ It's more interactive: read; pause to reflect, analyze, and discuss; then write down ideas, conclusions, and techniques which you can *apply*.

➤ Finally, the structure of this book leads to **action** by prompting you to compile these ideas, conclusions, and techniques into an **Action Plan** that improves your daily work and personal life—starting now.

There's an important assumption that flows throughout this book: **your attitude belongs to you.** It's what *you* decided it is, not what anyone else says it "should be." Changes you make are changes which *you* decide to make. Your attitude is *your* most priceless possession!

Wil McKnight

Acknowledgements

This book is dedicated to my dad, who, for nearly 90 years, has demonstrated the priceless benefit of a positive attitude, and to my friend, Laurene, who helped me get my attitude straightened around and focused on what's really important. "What counts can't be counted," she says.

Contents

Part 3: Attitude and Your Job

Part 4: Protecting Your Most Priceless Possession

Summary

PART 1

Understanding Your Attitude

What Is a Positive Attitude?

Attitude is your general disposition—your mental "starting point" for viewing life and the people and events in it. From your viewpoint, attitude is the way you look at things mentally, and it all starts inside *your head.* For others, *your attitude* is the overall mood they interpret from what they see you say and do.

People usually respond favorably to a positive attitude, and an optimistic person who always seems to anticipate good news transmits a positive attitude. People who expect the worst project a negative attitude that "speaks" louder than anything they say. And, it's a natural response for others to shy away from people who might make them feel negative.

Think of attitude as your *mental focus* on the world around you. When using a camera or camcorder, you can focus it on whatever you want. You can focus or set your mind in the same way—to see either opportunity or trouble. A difficult task is something to complain about or it's an opportunity to show what you or your staff can do. A regular staff meeting is a chance to solve a problem, develop an idea, communicate information—or it can become a gripe session.

Perception—the complicated process of viewing the world and interpreting the view—is a mental activity that's full of choices. It's within your power to concentrate on some aspects of your world and set others aside. Quite simply, you run the camera and take the picture of life that you want to take.

Emphasizing the positive is like using a magnifying glass:

➤ Place the glass over good news and feel better;

➤ Or magnify bad news and make yourself (and others) feel miserable.

And, what each person chooses to magnify can become a habit. Continually focusing on the bad news often exaggerates the negative impact of problems.

Another approach is to imagine that you have binoculars. Use them in the conventional way to view positive things, bringing them closer and into sharp focus. But flip them around and put the big lens to your eye to view bad news. You'll still be aware of problems, but they won't loom quite so large. By adjusting your mental image of a situation to highlight the positive, you'll often find that you're in a better position to deal with it, even if it's a difficult or troublesome situation.

"I've learned that most of the things I worry about never happen."

–H. Jackson Brown, Jr.

Your Attitude Is Never Static

Your attitude can be affected by everything around you. Events, people, and circumstances bring a steady stream of positive and negative factors or messages into your thoughts and feelings every day. So, your attitude is usually in flux—the result of an on-going process that is dynamic and sensitive to what's going on.

It's wise to be on guard so negative factors don't slip in and dominate your perspective, causing you to spend excessive "mind time" on difficulties rather than opportunities and solutions. If negative factors stay around long enough or if you become preoccupied with them, they will be reflected in "your attitude" as viewed by others. The positive will still be there, but it will be overshadowed by the negative.

Of course, no one can be 100% positive all the time because everyone receives a daily mixture of positive and negative factors or messages. Excessive optimism is unrealistic, and anyone who makes a noisy display of excessive optimism will probably be considered a fool or someone who's lost touch with reality. A positive attitude is not an act; it's a genuine way of viewing your life—and the people, events, and circumstances in your life.

Factors and Messages You've Encountered

Think back over the past week and recall various positive factors or messages and negative factors or messages you've encountered—at work and in your personal life. List as many of them as you can remember below. In Part 2 of this book, you'll learn ways to control or influence *the effect* of factors and messages on your attitude.

Positive factors or messages encountered at work	Negative factors or messages encountered at work
Positive factors or messages encountered in personal life	Negative factors or messages encountered in personal life

A Positive Attitude Is Worth Some Time and Trouble

Sometimes, when things get really tough, a positive attitude may be difficult to maintain—and inappropriate to display. But, day-in and day-out, it's worth it to treat a positive attitude as your #1 asset.

When things are going well, a positive attitude seems to feed on itself, and it's easy to maintain. But you're human, which means that you can expect people, events, or circumstances to test your positive mind-set. From time to time, some person or situation will pop up to step on your attitude and challenge your ability to bounce back.

When your attitude takes a hit, it's important to regain a positive frame of mind quickly. People who are unable to bounce back—they drag out misfortune or dwell on bad news—often find that their ability to work effectively and their relationships with others both suffer.

Part 2 of this book presents eight ways to maintain and recapture a positive attitude.

Diane Starts Each Day with a Positive Focus

The first thing Diane, a teller supervisor for a large bank, does when she wakes up each morning is to focus her mind on something positive—usually her "To Do" lists for yesterday and today. This gets her up on the "right side of the bed" by fixing her attention on yesterday's achievements and on the work she plans to accomplish today. Diane continues this practice throughout the day by actively looking for positive results from each person she works with. Because she's always looking for good news, she often finds it. What she views (takes into her mind), reinforces her positive attitude. Diane is frequently asked: "How come you're always so upbeat?"

Diane does not work for the Heavenly Bank & Trust, and she has her share of challenges and opportunities like most people who work in banking. Her effort to stay positive doesn't mean she ignores or avoids problems. It simply means she works to make the most out of each day. She moves quickly—and with a smile—to solve problems as they surface, rather than allowing them to drag her down with an "I'm a victim" attitude. She knows that simply having a positive attitude will not solve her problems or make difficult decisions unnecessary. However, a positive attitude puts her in a better frame of mind to sort out the facts, identify the real issue, find a good solution, and put it in place.

Diane is always thinking up and forward. And, she's moving up and forward too; she's been promoted twice in the last three years.

A Positive Attitude Makes Problem Solving Easier

Business is competitive and it usually moves fast for everyone, no matter where you are on the organization chart. *Everyone!* If your job includes managing or supervising people or decision making of any kind, dealing with problems that need to be solved is simply part of "what you do" every day. A positive attitude is part of the foundation that enables you to address a problem and take effective action to solve it. If you lose touch with your positive attitude, problem solving becomes more difficult and sometimes impossible.

You've probably seen this happen: someone with a negative attitude confronts a problem by chasing symptoms instead of identifying the real problem; they focus on blame instead of solutions; the cooperation of others they need for implementing a solution is sometimes damaged. Their negative attitude turns a typical day-to-day problem into a trouble spot that stays touchy for days. The same problem—if addressed with a positive attitude—could have been solved by four o'clock, and everyone would have felt good about it. The difference—and it was a negative difference—was all in the problem solver's attitude.

Juan's Attitude Helps Him Stay Focused

Although it wasn't easy, Juan became a department head this year. It wasn't easy, because for four years, Juan worked as a supervisor for a department head who didn't accept him and often gave him a hard time. When asked how he managed to remain positive under such uncomfortable circumstances, Juan replied: "My goal has always been to become a department head.

"I decided to do my best to be cooperative and as friendly as possible no matter what he dished out. I also tried to focus on the results my staff was supposed to achieve, and I took several courses at the community college so I could learn how to do my job better. On a day-to-day basis, though, I just tried to stay positive and keep my eye on my goal."

The High Expectancy Success Theory

It may sound too simple to say that "you see what you want to see." Yet, some people look at a complex project or a difficult task and see only trouble—budget problems, scheduling conflicts, turf battles, and other complications; others know they might have to deal with problems like these, but they see through them. They see solutions—and they *expect* to see solutions. Some can turn a scheduling problem into a customer service opportunity. A few will see the potential in a skilled but volatile associate that others cannot. In many ways and situations, the camera is in your hands, and you will see what you choose to see.

The High Expectancy Success Theory produces effective results for many people. This idea states that the more you **expect** from a situation, the more **success** you will achieve. It is a variation of the self-fulfilling prophecy. However, remember that it cuts both ways; if you expect failure, you increase your chance of realizing failure.

A new or inexperienced employee who arrives at the office each day *expecting to do good work,* will often have a more productive impact than a senior staffer who simply shows up and goes through the motions.

The High Expectancy Success Theory has a sound foundation. When you focus on the possibility of success, your senses become sharper, your enthusiasm is released, and you'll come closer to reaching your potential. You simply won't get the same results if you just expect to "sneak by."

Chantel Bootstraps Her Attitude

Normally a positive person, Chantel was thrown for a loop when her best friend, Tori, told her about some serious difficulties at home. It wasn't Chantel's problem, but for weeks she wallowed in a daze. Instead of locking in on the positive elements in the situation—Tori and her family were working through the difficulties—Chantel saw only the negative. Although she didn't recognize it at the time, Chantel was going through a deep and painful attitude adjustment—in a negative direction.

It wasn't until she became involved in some diversionary activities—helping her son with a special school project and resuming her regular aerobics class at the gym—that Chantel was able to shift her mental attention back to more positive things and regain her positive attitude. She eventually won this difficult battle and most aspects of her life began to feel good again. Her friends, especially Tori, were glad when she bounced back.

And, Chantel learned another lesson from this experience: a positive attitude can only be regained through conscious effort. When something jars your mental focus in a negative direction, you must make some sort of adjustment—*take action*—to get back on track. A positive attitude won't be rekindled through spontaneous combustion; you'll have to relight the fire.

 Special note: The examples and cases in this book are intended to present situations within the "nomal range" that most people can expect to encounter. They are not intended to portray serious cases of depression or other emotional difficulties for which professional assistance is appropriate or required.

The Importance of a Positive Attitude

Most business is complex and competitive, and it moves along swiftly—there's always time pressure. Your company wins many sales and customers, but you don't win them all. Your competitors aren't fools—in fact, some of them are pretty sharp—and most parts of the playing field are level. Good resources are available to everyone: good facilities, equipment, suppliers, vendors, and up-to-date technology. Everyone draws from the same labor pool; there are first-rate people in every company. So, what can make a difference? Where does your company get an edge?

Attitude Makes a Difference

Working with people who have a good attitude is like running with the wind at your back. Working with people who have a negative attitude is like a Friday afternoon commute in the rain—it takes more energy, more time, and there's always a greater chance that something bad will happen.

People with a good attitude always seem to be looking up and looking forward. People who are looking up and looking forward...

> ➤ See more opportunities and are more likely to spot problems in time to avoid major consequences.

> ➤ Are more likely to work to higher standards of quality, safety, and productivity.

> ➤ Are always looking out for other people, and this teamwork improves overall quality, safety, and productivity.

> ➤ Are more desirable to work with—and the work is more enjoyable.

> ➤ Are more likely to be promoted to more responsible jobs; they are more likely to move up and forward.

A goal of this book is to help you become someone who can:

➤ See opportunities;

➤ Spot problems in time to take action and avoid major consequences;

➤ Look out for your customers, your co-workers, yourself, and your company on every project or activity you're involved with;

➤ Enjoy your work;

➤ Move as far up and forward as you want.

The attitude you bring with you every day will significantly affect what you can see, what you can do, and how you feel about it. Read on. You'll see.

 When a positive attitude ripples through a department or a project or a company, it is a more powerful force than any budget, any schedule, any slogan or business plan—and it has a much greater effect on performance than any kind of top-down pressure because **it flows from within each person.**

A Positive Attitude Affects Personality

Personality is often defined as the unique mix of physical and mental traits found in an individual. For example, if you combine a person's physical characteristics (eyes, smile, posture, etc.) and mental characteristics (intelligence, tact, tolerance, determination, etc.), the sum total is that individual's personality.

Your personality also exists in the minds of others—and is defined by each of them according to the way they view you. The way other people interpret your personality is a key factor in how they relate to you. And, their interpretation is not based on what you think you are, it's based on what *they* think you are.

Sometimes the term *charisma* is used to describe someone's personality. A small percentage of people seem to be able to capture the imagination of others and inspire commitment to a higher cause or goal. Some people in leadership roles also seem to have charisma, but most of us don't. We simply do the best we can with what we've got—and personality is an important part of "what we've got."

A Positive Attitude and Your Personality

The impact of attitude is so great that it can overshadow the physical and mental characteristics within a personality. A positive attitude can be powerful enough to enhance personality traits. On the other hand, a negative attitude can diminish or cover up what would otherwise be attractive personal characteristics. It's too much to say a positive attitude can create charisma—but it can lift anyone's personality to a more attractive level:

➤ A person with a highly positive attitude can convert an ordinary personality into one that is interesting or exciting to others.

➤ A positive attitude can make a typical person seem better looking to others.

➤ A positive attitude can attract attention to outstanding traits in a personality that would normally go unnoticed.

➤ Some positive attitudes seem to "shine through" other personality characteristics, making the total image of the person brighter and more attractive to others.

There's little question that a positive attitude can help you make the most of your personality. Many talented people—including some with highly desirable traits and even charisma—can be lonely or unhappy, both on the job and in their personal lives—because they don't realize the importance of a positive attitude. They depend too heavily on their attractive physical or mental characteristics: talent, intelligence, appearance, education, family, or position. They forget that others prefer to be around and work with people who are positive.

Lisa and Stacy Discover the Effect of Personality

Lisa, an associate for a large, national retailer, grew up feeling she had a so-so personality. Her smile was pleasant but she was never the life of the party. Her other traits were not outstanding enough to keep her from getting lost in the crowd. Then Lisa discovered that people treated her a little differently when she focused on the interesting and challenging side of her job. This focus led her to reflect a highly positive attitude—first about her work and later about her life in general. Soon she was receiving compliments on personal characteristics that people had never noticed before.

Stacy was considered by others to be a successful office manager, with a lot of skill and drive. Even so, she was not popular. One co-worker said about Stacy: "She's got it all, but somehow she always manages to show the rest of us her worst side." Later, after Stacy completed a training course on leadership skills, she seemed to change. She began listening more to her staff, praising their good work, and looking for positive things. Soon she was getting positive responses from all directions. When asked what could cause such an upbeat change in her behavior, Stacy replied: "It's simple. I finally discovered there's a connection between my attitude and my desire to do a good job. When I approach things with a positive attitude, my whole staff is more productive, and we all seem to enjoy the work more."

A Change in Your Attitude Can Change the Way People View Your Personality

You may have noticed that a friend or co-worker suddenly seems more pleasant to be around without winning the lottery, getting a promotion, or any other special occasion or recognition. How could this happen? A new—and more positive—attitude might be responsible.

Most of us must learn to live comfortably with our inherited traits, characteristics, and limits. We can make improvements through diet, exercise, learning new skills, and by gaining experience. But after doing our best in these areas, we recognize that further improvements in the way others view us must come primarily through a better projection of the qualities we already possess.

The way to project the best possible personality is through a positive attitude!

The Power of a Positive Attitude

Using the word *power* to emphasize the effect of a positive attitude might seem like an overstatement. Yet, if you've been a close observer of people and their behavior, you've probably seen the effect of an attitude "turn-around" that was so extraordinary that the word *powerful* would be the only way to describe it.

If you have a positive attitude, its effect will show up in other important ways. Three advantages of a positive attitude are described on the following pages. Read about them and, at the end of each section, indicate whether you agree or disagree.

Advantage 1: A Positive Attitude Triggers Your Enthusiasm

You've probably seen this happen: someone becomes negative and they just seem to lose their energy. Their posture sags, and they often drag around the office as if their shoes were made of lead. In contrast, you've probably also seen people who are positive, with energy that appears to be endless.

John Goes Into a Funk

Two months ago, John made an expensive mistake on one of his project budgets, and his manager became annoyed and heavy-handed. Even though John corrected the problem and made up most of the deficit the next month, it was a visible blunder, and everyone in the department knew about it. Some people distanced themselves from him. And, recognizing his own stupidity, John came down hard on himself. His long-term career goals suddenly seemed impossible. He lost his self-confidence.

In short, John allowed one negative experience to change his focus on life. Only 27 years old and in excellent health, he plodded around the office—languid, looking weary, and "burned out." John's boss, who had forgotten all about the incident, worried that John might be physically ill.

Today John is back on track and views his career with enthusiasm. His friends and colleagues have reconnected with him now that he's optimistic and self-confident. John's new energy surfaced because his manager invited him to talk about what was bothering him. Through this counseling, John concluded that it was stupid to shackle himself with a negative attitude because of one mistake.

Observation: John's lack of enthusiasm was not due to illness, diet, something in his DNA, or his environment. It was simply a negative attitude. When John was able to recapture his positive focus, he automatically became more energetic. His reservoir of enthusiasm was there all the time. It just needed to be released again.

Do you... ❐ Agree   ❐ Disagree   Why?

_____

_____

_____

Advantage 2: A Positive Attitude Enhances Your Creativity

Being positive helps your mind think about opportunities and solutions more freely. One positive idea often leads to another. On the other hand, a negative attitude has a stifling effect. One doomsday forecast often leads to another, and creative thinking about solutions is crowded out.

Pete Runs Out of Ideas

Pete is a copywriter for a medium-sized ad agency. His agency's specialty is industrial product launches that are generally complex because of the technical specs of the products and the media schedules required. Over the past five years, the company has grown about 15% per year, and Pete has been an important contributor by figuring out new strategies and by challenging "the way we've always done it." His ideas have also reduced overhead by creating a systematic approach to several key day-to-day tasks.

But, a few months ago, Pete had a tough setback in his personal life that affected his overall attitude. It's negative; he knows it and so does everyone else. On the last two proposals, to a hospital chain and a high-tech start-up, Pete's approach to the hospital's specs and the start-up's media schedule was conventional, not innovative, and the agency lost both projects. Many factors were involved, but Pete knows that the kind of creative ideas he used to generate would have improved his agency's position on both proposals.

If Pete can find a way to adjust his attitude back to positive, he'll probably regain his ability to come up with creative, bid-winning ways to do the work—approaches that are both realistic for the client and profitable to the agency.

Do you… ❏ Agree ❏ Disagree Why?

If you've seen situations where a positive attitude has enhanced creativity or a negative attitude has dampened it, briefly describe them below.

_____

_____

_____

Advantage 3: A Positive Attitude Makes Good Things Happen

It often seems that people who have a positive attitude have a tendency to make valuable or positive discoveries by accident. For them, "good stuff" just shows up—and it appears far more frequently than expected. This phenomenon is called serendipity, and somehow their vision cuts through and they repeatedly stumble across good news, solutions, and opportunities. Many people with a positive attitude wake up most mornings thinking: "Something good is probably going to happen to me today."

Do you... ❐ Agree   ❐ Disagree   Why?

_____

_____

_____

Likewise, serendipity seems to have a flip side for people who have a negative attitude. They have a tendency to make troublesome or negative discoveries by accident. It often seems that when the sky falls, they're under it. Many people with a negative attitude wake up with an uneasy feeling about what lies ahead.

Do you... ❐ Agree   ❐ Disagree   Why?

_____

_____

_____

It's a recurring theme in this book that your attitude is largely controllable—that you can propel it in either a positive or negative direction by what you think about and what you do. Therefore, if a positive attitude can lead to accidental, positive discoveries, you've nothing to lose by making an effort to retain or recapture a positive attitude.

If you've seen a situation where a positive attitude has enabled someone (including you) to make a valuable or positive discovery by accident, describe it below.

_____

_____

_____

Keeping Your Attitude at Peak Power

Enthusiasm, creativity, and serendipity are *results*. This means that they don't happen spontaneously, they're driven by your attitude and your actions. *Your actions flow from your attitude.* So, the first step is to put a positive attitude in place.

Once you develop a positive attitude, it makes sense to take steps to safeguard it— and every now and then, to also give it a tune-up.

Safeguarding Your Attitude

What are some of your most important assets? Perhaps your car, your computer, a boat or camper, a stereo—items that can easily be stolen. When you think of your positive attitude as an asset, does it occur to you that your attitude can also be stolen? It happens all the time.

Grand Theft Attitude

Jay, a respected salesman for a regional printer, thought his working relationship with GenCo was pretty solid, but he got the shock of his life when GenCo switched its annual report to a competitor. Not only did the loss of this major project mean a reduction in income for Jay, but it tarnished his image in his three-state market. He complained and moped about the incident for weeks. Eventually, he became so negative that GenCo took him off their preferred list, and it was downhill after that. Jay turned in his car last week. Not only did his competitor "steal" a key project, but Jay allowed his positive attitude to be "stolen" as well.

About a month ago, Liz, a claims administrator in the home office of a large insurance company, got into an argument with Ted, a branch manager in another time zone. She unloaded a ton of stored-up grievances. When the incident was over, rather than clearing up the matter and trying to restore their relationship, Liz continued to stew over it and eventually her attitude turned negative. Liz allowed this unresolved conflict to "steal" her positive attitude, and it affected her work with several other branch managers in that region.

Heather and Brian had been going together for about a year when it became obvious that things weren't going to work out. After several recent disagreements and heated arguments, they split up. It became painfully obvious to her friends and family that Heather's attitude had turned negative. As often happens, Heather carried her negative attitude to work. After a couple of weeks of tension, her friend and co-worker, Nancy remarked: "Face it, Heather, you've put all the blame on Brian, and you've become angry and vindictive. Brian's history now, so don't let him steal your positive attitude on his way out the door."

Theft Prevention: Safeguarding Your Attitude

Unpleasant events and conflicts with other people, both on and off the job, can disrupt your work, affect your personal life, and undermine your general feeling about yourself. If you allow others to disrupt you to the point that you lose your positive approach to life, you've let things go too far. But what can you do to prevent others from stealing your positive attitude? Following are three ideas to consider whenever events or other people cause a challenge to your positive attitude.

Idea 1: Solve Personal Conflicts Quickly

In business and personal life, problems that come up seldom solve themselves–they may fester and get worse, and sometimes with the passing of time, solutions that might have worked earlier become unavailable. This applies to technical problems, marketing difficulties, and *especially* conflicts between people.

If you have a conflict with someone, you may feel better if you take the initiative to deal with it, even if you feel the other person is more responsible for the situation than you are. This may lead you to make an apology that you don't really want to make, initiating a discussion that you'd rather put off, or it may even mean swallowing some of your pride. But, if you allow a small problem to grow, it can eventually cause you to lose your positive attitude.

If possible, try not to carry over conflicts from one day to the next, and also try very hard not to carry over conflicts from Friday to Monday. The tension that accompanies an unresolved conflict can eat away at your positive attitude, and the longer it eats away, the more you stand to lose.

Idea 2: When People Behave Unreasonably or Unfairly, Take the High Road; Don't Drop to Their Level

Obviously, there are important issues and values where you have to take a stand. But, most conflicts or situations don't call for full-bore retaliation. When someone behaves unreasonably or unfairly, stop for a moment and remember: **you have a choice**. Often it's better to back off–especially if retaliation means that you'll get so upset or focused on "getting even" that the process might turn your attitude negative.

If you're a supervisor, your job is *to get results by working **through** other people*. If you're not a supervisor, your job is *to get results by working **with** other people*. So, when you stop for a moment, try to think about the long term results you want–including the effect on your attitude–in addition to what you want right now. Include both viewpoints when you decide how to respond to someone who acts unreasonably or unfairly. If you're uncertain, take the high road first and see how that approach works out.

 How many times can you go "an eye for an eye" with somebody? After twice, aren't you both blind? If so, who wins?

Idea 3: When You Have Repeated Conflicts with Someone, Insulate or Distance Yourself

If your relationship with someone repeatedly turns your attitude negative, the only way to recapture your positive attitude may be to put some distance between yourself and that person. In your personal life, putting distance or even making a complete withdrawal is difficult, but in a work relationship it's often impossible—unless, of course, you can transfer to another project or move to another company.

More likely, you'll have to deal with the situation without moving very far from your normal base. But, there are two approaches you can consider, and maybe one or both of them will help:

➤ **Focus on the work.** You can *focus on the results* you're expected to obtain. If you turn out first-rate work day after day, you'll be less likely to turn your attention to this person or the conflict itself. You may not increase the actual distance between the two of you, but it will seem like you have.

➤ **Change your traffic pattern.** Even if you're in the same building or in the same office, you probably have some freedom to move around and some choices. If you don't have to work directly with or consult this person, don't. Many work-related conversations are a mixture of business and personal exchanges; you can be all business. You can cut out any social interaction.

Of course, you don't want to insulate yourself from anyone by hiding, but you can make sure you don't go out of your way to maintain or reduce the distance between you.

These three ideas can also apply to events and conflicts in your personal life. Be aware that most of the time, your attitude—whether it's positive or negative—commutes right along with you.

Remember: Your Attitude Belongs to You

Keep in mind that your attitude belongs to you and to you alone. It's of no use to others. If they "steal" your positive attitude, they can't use it to become more positive themselves. Attitude theft is not a zero sum game–there's a loser and no winner. All an attitude thief can do is cause you damage.

But, you don't have to let them. No one can steal your positive attitude unless you are an accomplice.

Do you...   ❒ Agree   ❒ Disagree   Why?

_____

_____

A Note About Case Studies

The purpose of a case study is to provide insights you may not otherwise gain by just reading about ideas and skills. Five case studies are included in this book to present specific situations to think about and to show how you can *apply* important ideas and skills to real business and personal situations.

These cases don't have exact solutions or answers. Different points of view are always possible–and even encouraged–in discussions of people, their attitudes, and their behavior. You can benefit two ways:

➤   First, by analyzing the case and expressing your views; then

➤   By comparing your ideas with the suggested responses and solutions shown on page 98.

Please understand that it's not our intent to stereotype any person, any group, or any business segment or industry by our choice of language or by the circumstances described in the case studies and anecdotes presented in this book. These brief examples are intended to present situations within the "normal range" that most people can expect to encounter. They are not intended to portray serious cases of depression or other emotional difficulties for which professional assistance is appropriate or required.

Case Study 1: Maria's Mood Swings

Maria, a Registered Nurse, is trying hard to make the most out of life—she is doing her best to be a first-rate professional, a good wife and mother, and an active community member. Her last check-up was excellent; she manages a brisk 20 minute walk a couple of times a week and generally takes pretty good care of herself.

But for some reason, Maria has major mood swings. She explains: "I'm either up or down. Some days I feel like I've got it made in the shade. Other days I'm down and I know it. Everyone says it's not serious, just a matter of attitude. But, little things seem to tip me one way or another. Like when the weather is bad, my attitude tumbles. When one of my kids gets sick, my attitude drops. When the bills pile up like they did after the holidays, my attitude is in the dumpster."

Assume you and Maria work on the same shift, and you often have lunch together. You would like to help her reduce her mood swings. How would you go about doing this?

_____

_____

_____

_____

_____

_____

_____

_____

_____

_____

_____

When you've finished analyzing the case and writing down your ideas and views, see **Comments on the Cases** in the back of this book for important ideas and insights about this case.

Attitude Renewal:
How to Give Your Attitude a Tune-Up

Everyone—employee, manager, owner, student, retiree—occasionally needs some kind of attitude renewal or attitude adjustment. There is no escape; nobody's attitude is permanently set.

Attitude renewal means to restore or refresh your viewpoint; to rejuvenate your approach; to re-establish your positive focus; to repair the wear and tear to your attitude. Attitude renewal is like a tune-up.

Weekends, holidays, and vacations are frequently used as "pit stops" for attitude renewal. These breaks are necessary to combat the daily stress and strain that everyone encounters.

Environmental shock waves. As a seismograph records the intensity and duration of an earthquake, your attitude reflects tremors caused by financial tensions, personal disappointments, family problems, health concerns, work and personal pressures, and so on. There is no way to fully insulate yourself from these shock waves.

Self-image problems. From time to time—for any number of reasons—you might feel you don't look or feel quite as sharp as you once did. This creates a negative self-image—a kind of "dirty shirt feeling" that can keep you from thinking of your-self in a positive way. When this happens, doing something to improve your self-image can make a difference. Health clubs, clothing stores, beauty salons, Ed's Barber Shop—all can be attitude adjustment stations.

Negative drift. Nobody can explain why it happens, but sometimes, even when things are going smoothly, you sort of feel yourself drifting toward a negative attitude. Some blame this kind of drift on all the negative information that seems to fill drive-time radio, the newspapers, cable news and "news" talk shows, and much of primetime TV. If the messages from mass media sort of make you feel that the world is drifting in a negative direction, your attitude, if you let it, may drift right along with it.

Daily Adjustments

Attitude renewal at the first level is a daily process. For some, a few moments of quiet or meditation seems to make a difference. Others get squared away with a more businesslike approach; they feel on top of things when they get a handle on the day by getting organized. Still others listen to special music or motivational tapes on the way to or from work.

Such minor adjustments can happen anytime or anyplace, but the beginning and the end of the day seem to be the most effective times. For some people, daily attitude adjustment is a solitary process; others share their thoughts and feelings with another person. Each person finds out what works through trial and error.

Weekend Tune-Ups

At the next level, attitude renewal can be a "weekend project." "I use weekends for recreation. By Monday morning I'm rested and positive." "The quiet time during church each Sunday is a wonderful way to regroup for the week ahead." "Without weekends to unwind, I'd be a burnout candidate."

Weekends offer a change of pace, a change of scenery, and also opportunities to spend time with a different group of people. Weekends offer a chance to catch up on work, to catch up on rest, or to recharge whatever resources have been run down the hardest during the past few days. However, weekend attitude renewal doesn't happen automatically. It's far more effective if you think about it some and plan some part of your weekend with the *intention* of renewing your attitude.

Getting Out of a Rut

Daily and weekend activities can help you keep your equilibrium from week to week. There are times, however, when a major overhaul is necessary. Occasionally, you may find yourself in a serious attitudinal "rut." You're in a rut when you repeat a pattern of negative behavior for a period of time. Although some days are better than others, your focus seems permanently skewed to the negative side.

It's possible to be in such a rut without knowing it. When you become physically ill, for example, your body normally send signals—you get a headache, a fever, or a pain. This alert prompts you to do something about the illness. However, when you slip into an attitudinal rut, your mind may be unable to send you a signal; or, you may refuse to receive it. Your friends might say something or they might hold back because they fear an angry response. Or they send signals that you ignore. So, it's not unusual for people to stay in an attitudinal rut for longer than necessary.

Don Falls Into a Rut

Over a year ago Don fell into a negative rut when he was passed over when his department head set up a special project team. He had worked hard and felt he deserved the assignment more than two of the persons selected. Don is still negative, but if you were to tell him his negative attitude shows, he'd deny it. He's been in a rut so long he thinks his behavior is normal.

The worst aspect of Don's situation is that his attitude has spilled over from work to his personal life, making things extremely difficult for his family.

If your job pushes you into a rut, it's likely you will extend it to other aspects of your life, especially your personal life. Unfortunately, it works the other way too. Negative effects from your personal life will probably surface in your attitude at work. Be on the lookout from both directions!

Good-bye, Mrs. Flint

Everyone at Willowbrook Middle School wishes Mrs. Flint would retire but she has at least another 10 years to go. At one time, students looked forward to her classes. Now they dread them and make nasty remarks barely out of earshot. Other teachers used to enjoy having lunch with her. Now she eats alone.

As far as anyone knows, nothing dramatic happened to cause Mrs. Flint to be in a negative rut. Apparently she simply drifted into it. Everyone was afraid to say anything to her about it, and she just sort of got sullen and stayed that way. She doesn't even realize her negative attitude is so noticeable. "I'm just getting old," she says. "I've been teaching too long."

Attitude knows no age level. Attitude adjustments are necessary at every age and every stage of life. It's possible to get *older* without getting *old*.

Use the attitude barometer on the next page to assess your current attitude. You can also pair up with a friend or co-worker to fill out this form for each other, and if you do, you might get a reality check—outside feedback to compare with your inside view of your attitude.

Attitude Barometer

Assess your current attitude by reading each statement and circling the number that you feel is an accurate description of your current attitude. A "10" means your attitude could not be better in this area; a "1" means it could not be worse. Be honest; no one is looking at this page but you. After you complete this exercise, check the interpretation of this attitude barometer.

< High............Low >
< Positive......Negative >

1. My guess is that my supervisor would rate my current attitude as a:　　10 (9) 8 7 6 5 4 3 2 1

2. My staff (or the people I work closest with) would probably rate my current attitude as a:　　(10) 9 8 7 6 5 4 3 2 1

3. My family would probably rate my current attitude as a:　　(10) 9 8 7 6 5 4 3 2 1

4. Honestly, I would rate my current attitude as a:　　10 9 8 (7) 6 5 4 3 2 1

5. In dealing with others, I believe my effectiveness would rate a:　　10 9 8 (7) 6 5 4 3 2 1

6. If there were a meter that could gauge my sense of humor, I believe it would read close to a:　　10 (9) 8 7 6 5 4 3 2 1

7. My recent disposition—the patience and sensitivity I show to others—deserves a rating of:　　10 (9) 8 7 6 5 4 3 2 1

8. When it comes to not allowing little things to bother me, I've recently earned a:　　10 (9) 8 7 6 5 4 3 2 1

9. Based upon the number of compliments I've received lately, I deserve a:　　10 9 (8) 7 6 5 4 3 2 1

10. I would rate my enthusiasm toward my job and my life during the past few weeks as a:　　10 9 (8) 7 6 5 4 3 2 1

Total _____

An Interpretation of the Attitude Barometer Scale

A total of 90 or over is a signal that your attitude is "in tune," and no adjustments seem necessary; a total between 70 and 90 indicates that minor adjustments may help; a total between 50 and 70 suggests a major adjustment; if you rated yourself below 50, a complete overhaul may be required.

Case Study 2: Rita vs. Dawn

Rita is an outstanding manager when it comes to setting priorities, following through on details and running a tight but comfortable ship. Employees say about Rita: "You can depend upon her to be consistent," "When you have a problem you can feel free to go to her and she'll listen." "Rita plays it safe with her superiors so they don't rock the boat for the rest of us." "She's a dedicated supervisor—knows how we do things around here and sticks to the rules."

Dawn is a so-so manager but an exceptional leader. She's full of creative ideas, has an upbeat, dynamic attitude and doesn't mind rocking the boat to gain acceptance for change. Her employees say about Dawn: "Things are never dull around here." "One of these days, management will either fire Dawn or promote her." "She's so active, positive and inspirational that we all work harder for her than we would for someone else." On the other hand, some also say: "Frankly, I'd prefer just a good, steady manager instead of Dawn. She takes too many risks."

Most management experts agree that it is possible to be an outstanding manager and a weak leader. They also say that strong, dynamic leaders—people who inspire and motivate others—are sometimes average managers.

If you were the CEO of a fast-growing organization, which person would you recruit for a department head? Why?

Dawn. _____

_____

_____

If you were the CEO of a stable organization, which person would you recruit for a department head? Why?

Dawn. _____

_____

_____

When you've finished analyzing the case and writing down your ideas and views, see **Comments on the Cases** in the back of this book for important ideas and insights about this case.

Key Points from Part 1

What Is a Positive Attitude? (page 3)

➤ Attitude is the way you look at things mentally, your *mental focus* on the world.

➤ Your attitude is never static; it's always in flux–the result of an on-going process that's dynamic and sensitive to what's going on.

➤ Events, circumstances, and messages–both positive and negative–can affect your attitude.

➤ No one can be positive all of the time.

➤ A positive attitude makes problem solving easier.

➤ The more you expect from a situation, the more success you will achieve (*The High Expectancy Success Theory*).

The Importance of a Positive Attitude (page 9)

➤ Business is complex and competitive, and most competitors have access to comparable resources, including people.

➤ A company gets its edge from its supervisors, from training it provides to each employee, and from the attitude of its people.

➤ People with a positive attitude always seem to be looking up and looking forward; individually and as a team, they are more likely to work to higher standards of quality, safety, and productivity.

➤ The attitude you bring with you every day will significantly affect what you can see, what you can do, and how you feel about it.

A Positive Attitude Affects Personality (page 11)

➤ A person with a highly positive attitude can convert an ordinary personality into one that is interesting or exciting to others.

➤ A positive attitude can make a typical person seem better looking to others.

➤ A positive attitude can attract attention to outstanding traits in a personality that would otherwise go unnoticed.

➤ Some positive attitudes seem to "shine through" other personality characteristics, making the total image of a person brighter and more attractive to others.

The Power of a Positive Attitude (page 13)

➤ Result 1: A positive attitude triggers your enthusiasm.

➤ Result 2: A positive attitude enhances your creativity.

➤ Result 3: A positive attitude prompts serendipity; people who have a positive attitude have a tendency to make valuable or positive discoveries by accident.

Safeguarding Your Attitude (page 18)

➤ Safeguard your attitude by:

 – Solving personal conflicts quickly

 – Taking the "high road" if someone behaves unreasonably or unfairly

 – Insulating or distancing yourself from a person with whom you have a repeated conflict

 – Focusing on the work

 – Changing your traffic pattern to avoid people who pull your attitude down

➤ Remember: your attitude belongs to you and to you alone.

Attitude Renewal: How to Give Your Attitude a Tune-Up (page 23)

➤ Refresh your view, rejuvenate your approach, re-establish your positive focus, and repair the wear and tear on your attitude by dealing with environmental shock waves, self-image problems, and negative drift.

➤ Make minor, daily adjustments—by meditating, thinking, getting organized, relaxing, talking with someone.

➤ Do a weekend tune-up to get a change of pace or a change of scenery; spend time with different people.

➤ Although a person can drift into a rut without realizing it, usually it takes **action** of some kind to recapture a positive attitude (such as one of the 8 attitude adjustment techniques presented in Part 2).

➤ Sometimes the reason people lack a positive attitude is simply that they don't realize that they have a negative attitude.

Take a Few Minutes to Reflect

You've just finished Part 1 of this book and should have plenty of ideas and things to think about. This is a good time to take a break just to go over what you've learned:

➤ Go back to the table of contents and look over the list of topics for Part 1.

➤ Skim through Part 1 and pay special attention to the notes and answers you've written in your book.

➤ As you go over these pages again, write down any new ideas that come to mind.

➤ Review the Key Points covered in Part 1.

➤ Finally, go back and look over your responses to the Attitude Barometer; if any of your responses seem too high or low, change them.

Now, move on to Part 2 to learn about eight techniques for adjusting your attitude.

Working through a book like this is a booster shot, not a vaccination. As you go back and review key ideas, **circle the page number** for any topic you might want to revisit later.

Eight Ways
to Adjust
Your
Attitude

Adjustment Technique 4:
The Flipside Technique

The pivotal factor between feeling positive or negative is often a sense of humor. Attitude and humor seem to feed off each other. The more you learn to develop your sense of humor, the more positive you will become. The more positive you become, the better your sense of humor. It's a happy arrangement.

Some people successfully use the "flipside technique" to maintain and enhance their sense of humor. When a "negative" enters their lives, they immediately flip the problem over (like you'd flip a pancake) and look for whatever humor may exist on the other side. When this is successful, these savvy survivors are able to minimize the negative impact the problem or event has on their positive attitude.

Jim Recycles the Debris into a Vacation

Jim was devastated when he walked into his apartment. Everything was in shambles, and he quickly discovered some valuable possessions were missing. After assessing the situation, he called Mary and left her a voicemail: "I think I've figured out a way for us to take that trip to Cancun. I've just been robbed, but at least my homeowner's is paid up. Come on over and help me make a list and clean up the mess—and bring the brochures."

Cheryl's Trapped in the Elevator

Cheryl's sense of humor helped turn a traumatic experience into a profitable one. Working past midnight on a presentation one night, she became stuck in the elevator. Rather than becoming negative by cursing her problem all night; she sat down, and laughed at what was an impossible situation. "It's a two story building; next time I'll take the stairs." She even got some sleep before Maintenance let her out early the next morning. Cheryl recalls: "Thanks to my sense of humor and a few prayers, I was able to deal with it. After that experience, everybody regards me as a person who can handle a difficult situation."

Humor in any form can help you resist negative forces. It can restore your perspective and help you maintain—or recapture—a more balanced and positive outlook on life.

How do you define a sense of humor? It's a state of mind—a mental focus—that encourages a person to think about lighter aspects in a situation that others might not see. It's a philosophy that says:

➤ *If you take life with too much gravity, it will pull you down.*

➤ *Most troubles aren't the end of the world; if you learn to laugh at yourself and your temporary predicament, it sometimes makes life easier.*

➤ *When things get really tough, send in the clowns.*

Kikka's Overtime; Cathy's Repair Bill

Kikka was upset when she got to work and saw the notice for a special Friday afternoon staff meeting. She knew they were already behind on the Web site project. To get back on track, they learned the project team would be working overtime for the next eight weeks, right up until Christmas, including Thanksgiving. When Kikka got home that night she told her husband about the overtime—but then added that it might be their best Christmas ever, with all the extra cash.

When the service manager handed Cathy her car repair bill, she was shocked and could hardly calm down enough to write the check. But then she overheard another customer say: "Yikes! What a bill! I guess my car doesn't love me anymore. Oh well, no one said this love affair would be cheap." That customer, Megan, had the remarkable habit of "flipping" bad news into a humorous vein—something she could handle. Cathy decided it might be an approach worth trying.

Incidents which you can improve with a positive spin or a humorous twist occur several times each day in your life. Most of these moments will pass you by unless you train yourself to see them. To help you do this, it might help to give this mindset a special name: *Funny Focus; Cosmic View; The Laugh Truck.* It may sound frivolous or corny, but it describes what some people actually do every day of their lives because it works for them.

"When it hits the fan, Tom seems to know just the right joke to break the tension; then he gets everybody thinking positively about how to solve the problem."

"Lori always adjusts more quickly because she has the ability to direct her wild and crazy mind to the funny side of any problem."

"Sam's a good guy to have on your team because he can find something humorous in any situation."

People who receive such compliments are always ready to take a ride in *The Laugh Truck*, creating a more positive perspective for themselves and others. This focus is their pain reliever for negative situations.

How can you improve your attitude through an active, accessible sense of humor? How can you develop a *Cosmic View* that will fall within your comfort zone? Consider these three ideas:

➤ *Humor is an inside job.* Humor is not something that is natural for one and unnatural for another. One person is not blessed with a pot full of humor while another is left empty. A sense of humor can be created and nurtured—but you have to be looking for humor in a situation to see it. With practice, anyone can develop a *Funny Focus.*

➤ *Laughter is therapeutic.* Negative emotions such as tension, anger, and stress can produce ulcers, headaches, and high blood pressure. Likewise, positive emotions such as laughter can relax nerves, improve digestion, and help blood circulation. Laughter sets many beneficial physiological systems in motion, and research shows it can give your immune system a boost. Of course, it's not appropriate to laugh away all serious problems, and laughter is not a solution itself. But, anytime you can laugh your way into a more positive focus, it will take some of the sting out of the problem.

➤ *The Laugh Truck can pull you out of the problem and into a solution.* Simply finding the humor in a situation won't solve a problem, but it can lead you in the right direction. Laughing can help you focus on a problem more clearly and develop a solution more quickly or effectively. Using the flipside technique starts the process.

So, give the flipside technique a try. To explore the potential of this approach, work through the flipside exercise on the next page.

Warning! Be sensitive and cautious in your use of humor: Be aware of the effect of your humor and laughter on others so you don't laugh or make jokes which might be inappropriate or offensive to someone. Laugh at the behavior, not the person. Don't use humor to laugh at everything and deny the reality of difficult circumstances or problems.

Flipside Exercise

Most problems have a flipside—a humorous side. In the boxes below, list one or two negative situations which you currently face. Examples might be a staff change, new supervisor, or a different work schedule. Or it might be a financial matter such as an accumulation of bills or an unexpected rent increase. Then, in the right-hand box, identify any humor you might generate on the flipside. This may be a little difficult to do at first, but remember, if this technique was easy, more people would use it naturally.

Situation	Flipside

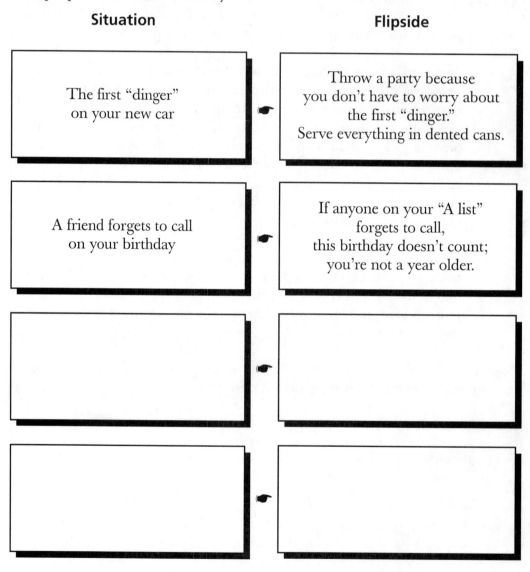

The first "dinger" on your new car

Throw a party because you don't have to worry about the first "dinger." Serve everything in dented cans.

A friend forgets to call on your birthday

If anyone on your "A list" forgets to call, this birthday doesn't count; you're not a year older.

Adjustment Technique 2:
Play Your Winners

When retailers discover that a certain item is a "hot seller," they pour additional promotional money into that product. "Play the winners—don't go broke trying to promote the losers," they say. This same approach can help you maintain or recapture a positive attitude. You have some special winners in your life. *The more you focus on these winners, the better.*

Julie Hangs in There

Julie, who handles claims for a large insurance company, has what she calls her "R&R times." Examples are watching old movies, doing aerobics, and getting together with friends over the grill and a few beers. But, Julie is also dealing with some negative factors. Right now, she's handling a tough claim on a multi-car accident, and lately she and her parents have gotten crosswise about a personal decision she made earlier this year. Yet she manages to remain positive most of the time, because she's learned how to play her winners.

Jake Turns the Corner and Sees Light Ahead

At this point, Jake has more losers than winners in his life. He's trying to lose 15 pounds; he can barely handle his monthly payments; and his car has developed a new death rattle. Two positive factors in his life are his job—he's just become a shift supervisor—and his running. By focusing his energy on his new work responsibilities plus running four miles a day, Jake has been able to maintain a positive attitude, and he dropped six pounds in the last three weeks. The car will have to wait until his new salary catches up with the payments, but this will happen in about three months. Jake is starting to feel okay about things. Jake feels this way because he's learned how to play his winners, though he'd be the first to tell you that it's not always easy to do.

All of us—at each stage in life—deal with both positive factors and messages (winners) and negative factors and messages (losers). If you're not alert, losers can push your winners to the background or even make them seem to disappear.

When this happens, it's possible to burn all your energy by dwelling on misfortunes and bad news. When the losers fester in your mind, your outlook will become increasingly negative, and your disposition will sour. You can affect this because you *have choices*: you can choose what you think about (thoughts) and you can choose what you do (action). Of course, sometimes you're sort of boxed in on a situation, *but your challenge is to find ways to push the losers into the background to make way for the winners.*

Think More about Your Winners

The more you concentrate on good news and the things you do well in life, the less time you'll have to think about the negative stuff. And, sometimes when negative factors and messages receive less attention, some of them resolve themselves—suggesting, perhaps, that they weren't that real or significant in the first place. For some people, most of the things they worry about never happen.

Nan's Daily Journal

Nan, a receptionist in the home office, keeps a diary about important events in her life. She makes it a point to pick out positive factors and messages when making entries in her diary. As she falls asleep at night, she thinks about new entries she'd like to make the next morning. Nan claims this technique helps her fall asleep faster, and gives her a better start on the next day. During a typical day, Nan talks to more than 200 people. Her positive attitude ripples throughout the office, to every branch and field rep, and it's also obvious to the company's suppliers and customers.

Talk about Your Winners

As long as you don't overdo it (or repeat yourself with the same person), the more you talk about the positive, exciting situations and events in your life, the more important they will become for you. Those who drag on about negative factors and situations perpetuate their own negative attitude—and eventually they discover that others are tired of hearing about it. They play their losers out loud—over and over—then they wonder why they're not winning and why nobody wants to listen anymore.

Reward Yourself by Enjoying Your Winners

If you enjoy working out or reading or talking with a special friend, make sure these activities are at the top of your weekly "To Do" list. If specific people are a positive influence, set aside time for them.

You play your winners every time you think or talk about them, but obviously the best approach is to enjoy them by taking **action**. If you enjoy fishing, an afternoon in a bass boat will do more for your attitude than telling old fish stories. If you enjoy movies, don't just read the reviews—go!

Like the Nike ad says: *Just Do It!*

Play Your Winners: An Exercise

List at least four positive factors or messages in your life—people, situations, events, activities or anything else that makes you feel positive. Where possible, use a single word or short phrase.

1. _____
   _____

2. _____
   _____

3. _____
   _____

4. _____
   _____

5. _____
   _____

6. _____
   _____

7. _____
   _____

8. _____
   _____

9. _____
   _____

You've just demonstrated that there are powerful positive factors and messages in your life. These are your winners. Play them!

Adjustment Technique 3:
Simplify! Simplify!

Some people gradually clutter their lives with minor negative factors and other complications that make it difficult for them to remain positive. They look up one day and discover that they've surrounded themselves with non-essential, high-maintenance possessions, people, or commitments. Then they complain about the complexity of their lives, time pressures, and the stress they feel.

Other people, while they don't reach this level of complexity and complaint, still become gradually entangled in a web of minor tasks, obligations, possessions, commitments, and involvements. They often feel bogged down—even though each one of these entanglements seemed like a good idea at the time.

The answer, of course, is to shed non-essential complications. An uncluttered life can allow you to notice and enjoy the things that are really important. To discover how you might simplify your life, read through the following five "clutter areas" and decide which of them apply to you. Clean out your clutter areas and you'll find more enjoyment in the people, activities, and commitments you decide to keep.

Clutter Area 1: Unused, Unappreciated, or Non-Essential Possessions

Some otherwise sensible people become slaves to their possessions. They surround themselves with more "stuff" than they need or have time to enjoy. Much of it is costly in time or trouble to keep or store. Every now and then you simply have to clean them out—because you can't find the tools you need, or you simply get tired of parking your car *in front* of the garage.

Take a walk around your house or apartment; check out the places where you stash "things you might need someday" and "things that don't work right but you paid too much to throw away." Notice those things that you once used but now sit idle—they've been outgrown or are simply not interesting anymore. Think about the "total cost" of keeping all of this "stuff"—the time, trouble, storage.

Maybe it's time to thin out your collection so you have more room for the items you really need and enjoy. Getting rid of things that are not essential can simplify your life—and improve your attitude—by creating more space for fewer essential possessions that you really value and enjoy.

❏ Clutter Area 1 applies to me   ❏ It doesn't apply to me

Possibilities: _____

_____

_____

Clutter Area 2: Too Many Commitments or Involvements

Some people, in their desire to "do good" or "look good," make more commitments than they can keep or take on more tasks than they can do well. As a result, their time and energy is consumed by others—other people, other organizations, other schedules and deadlines, other priorities and agendas.

Super Fred

Fred is so busy being a supervisor, a Sunday School teacher, a Little League coach, and a volunteer fireman he has forgotten how to have a good time. He's usually grouchy and impatient and is always running flat out. If he could settle for doing a solid, first-rate job in just two or three of these four areas, Fred would not only receive greater recognition, but it would also simplify his life. This would improve his attitude. It would be easier to be around Fred, even for Fred. Especially for Fred!

People who are generous with their time and talents sometimes don't realize that over-committing can negatively affect their attitude—and their behavior towards others. Consequently, their efforts, even when well-intended, can become counterproductive.

To see the scope of your commitments, list each one that requires more than three hours per week or 10 hours per month. Remember to also include the related time it takes for preparation, travel, clean-up, and other indirect tasks.

❏ Clutter Area 2 applies to me   ❏ It doesn't apply to me

Possibilities: _____

_____

_____

Clutter Area 3: Work-Home Imbalance

Some ambitious people devote so much time and energy to their work that they create tension in their personal or family relationships. These workaholics forget that an unhappy personal life can affect their overall attitude and cause them to turn negative on the job.

Lon and Larry Get Out of Balance

Lon is so committed to his job as branch manager that everything at home gets second priority. Although he tries to catch up on repairs and chores on Sundays, he never quite succeeds. As a result, family tensions sometimes run high and he feels frustrated. Lon can't seem to see that he could lower his frustration by shifting some time and attention to his personal life, and this would improve his attitude at work—and also improve his work performance.

Larry, one of Lon's key supervisors, is in two bowling leagues, works out three days a week, always seems to have "Somewhere I gotta go!" at 5:01 P.M., and hasn't missed a Monday Night Football game at the local sports bar in three years. His staff is often playing catch-up, and Larry spends a lot of time on the phone chasing down details and minor problems that should have been resolved yesterday. Larry doesn't seem to understand that successful supervisors often put in a longer work week than the staff that works for them.

Your personal life and your work life are linked—and the link is you. It can be a difficult balancing act, but it may be worthwhile for you to review your work and personal commitments, then simplify your life by shifting some of your time and energy from one to the other.

❑ Clutter Area 3 applies to me   ❑ It doesn't apply to me

Possibilities: _____

_____

_____

Clutter Area 4: Putting Off the Little Things

Most people have opportunities to remove minor negatives that enter their lives, but sometimes procrastinate and just put up with these trivial distractions. Eventually, an accumulation of minor negatives injures their outlook. You've seen situations like these:

➤ A minor physical problem that is eventually eliminated by a simple out-patient surgery;

➤ Putting off a simple car repair until it leads to a major problem, a significant expense, and a big frustration;

➤ Ignoring a 30-minute repair task until it becomes a major issue and the subject of a family argument.

Each life contains some minor, unpleasant tasks. Individually, they're trivial and probably not consequential, but if they pile up they can undermine your attitude.

❏ Clutter Area 4 applies to me   ❏ It doesn't apply to me

Possibilities: _____

_____

_____

Clutter Area 5: Holding on to Worn-Out Relationships

Some people have a few "friends" who are chronically negative and being around these "friends" pulls them down. It may sound harsh, but it's usually wise to put people like that at some distance—even if it means that you are the one who must give up an activity or make an adjustment to create the space.

And it's never easy, but in some cases, it's even necessary to break off a negative personal relationship to protect your attitude. If you find yourself in this situation, make the break directly, firmly, and without guilt. When the tension or sadness of the break-up moment passes, you'll notice an improvement in your attitude.

❏ Clutter Area 5 applies to me   ❏ It doesn't apply to me

Possibilities: _____

_____

_____

Simplification Exercise

Now, look back over your notes on Adjustment Technique 3 Simplify! Simplify! and make a short list of possibilities that you could realistically do within the next 30 days. Then circle three of them and say to yourself: "I promise to do these three things to simplify my life."

1. _____

_____

2. _____

_____

3. _____

_____

4. _____

_____

5. _____

_____

6. _____

_____

7. _____

_____

Today's Date: _____

 Sometimes it seems easier to limp along than to stop and take the time to remove a tiny pebble from your shoe.

Adjustment Technique 4:
Insulate! Insulate!

It's not realistic to think that all negative factors in our lives can be *eliminated* through any of the adjustment techniques suggested in this book. Everyone, at some point, must learn to live with certain "no-win" situations that cannot be easily eliminated, reduced, or avoided.

Almost everyone has worked for a difficult boss and survived. Others have managed to stay positive in spite of a chronic personal problem that can't be solved. Still others have found a way to cope in a positive manner despite a permanent illness or handicap.

What is the answer? *Work to insulate your focus against the negative factor.* Employ techniques which isolate or detach these negative factors so their effect on your attitude is minimized. Find ways to push them into the background, out of your focus, to keep them at bay.

Phase I Insulators

Here are nine kinds of adjustments people often make to keep a major negative factor under control. Think of them as Phase I insulators:

- ➤ Keep busy
- ➤ Adopt a "one day at a time" philosophy
- ➤ Play your winners
- ➤ Exercise
- ➤ Use humor
- ➤ Simplify your life
- ➤ Concentrate on positive thoughts
- ➤ Do something for someone else
- ➤ Spend time with a friend

Phase II Insulators

Long-term problems have a way of laying dormant for awhile, then popping to the surface with a vengeance, causing the loss of a positive focus. Sometimes these problems reach crisis proportions.

What adjustments can one make when serious problems flare up or the calendar prompts a difficult part of the past to reappear? Phase I techniques are helpful, but sometimes more drastic adjustments are required. Here are five different ways people deal with such situations. The purpose of these Phase II insulators is to keep the problem in perspective while one works on solutions or learns to cope.

Toni Talks It Out

Whenever Toni faces a recurring problem, she makes her attitude adjustment primarily through long discussions with her husband or her close friends, Erica and Josie. She deflates the problem to a manageable size by getting it out of her system—like letting air out of a balloon.

"I learned long ago that I need to talk out major problems to put them into perspective. It's sometimes a little hard on Tom and my friends, but I pay them back by listening when they need to talk."

Mario Works It Out

You can always tell when Mario is dealing with a big problem by the intensity of his off-the-job physical activities.

"Hard work has always been therapeutic for me. When I'm faced with a difficult situation, you'll find me cleaning out the garage, clearing brush, or working out. When I pour my sweat and energy into an unrelated job, my problem seems to get smaller, and then I can do something about it."

Michelle Laughs It Out

Michelle deals with no-win problems by refusing to take them too seriously. This approach—a kind of psychological immunity—seems to protect her positive attitude.

"I know it sounds crazy; but, when I can't deal in a normal way with one of my problems, I do bizarre things like rollerblading to work or wearing my special black headband until I've made an adjustment. I joke around some until the problem seems more manageable."

Bert Prays about It

Whenever one of Bert's chronic problems resurfaces, he relies on prayer. If this doesn't cut it to size, he seeks counsel with his pastor.

"God and I are partners. I do His work as a mortal, and then call on Him when I need help. It's a terrific arrangement, and it's never let me down."

Kelly Changes the Scene

When an "old problem" starts to nag Kelly, she goes to the lake where she claims a new perspective is possible.

"When the going gets rough, I'm gone. I isolate for a while. I don't stay away too long, but a change of scene with nobody else around pulls my focus back to the positive side, and I can cope with it. Don't ask me why–this just works for me."

Develop Your Own Personal Program

Each person must design his or her own attitude adjustment program. The combination that works for one person may not be effective for another. The Insulation Checklist exercise below may help you figure out what works for you.

Insulation Checklist

The suggestions below may help you insulate your attitude against negative factors which are outside your control. Read the complete list and place the number 1 on the line opposite the suggestion you like best, number 2 on the line of the idea you like second best, etc., and continue until you have your own "package" of approaches listed in priority order.

_____ Refuse to assume responsibility for other peoples' problems

_____ Put limits on your involvement in the negative drama of others

_____ Play your winners; concentrate on factors which are positive for you

_____ Find ways not to worry about things beyond your control

_____ Share your problems with God

_____ Talk over the problem with a trusted friend or a professional counselor

_____ Use the "flipside" technique; keep things light

_____ Keep busy; work out problems through physical activity

_____ Make a temporary change in your environment–take a long drive or a mini-vacation

_____ Do something to help others

_____ Engage in a special leisure activity (a hobby, sports, running, hiking, etc.)

_____ Other:

Adjustment Technique 5:
Give Your Positive Attitude to Others

When you're frustrated by the behavior of others, you may be tempted to give them "a piece of your mind" or simply withdraw and let your attitude sag. It's a better approach, however, to turn around and give someone else "a piece of your positive attitude." When you do this, you'll find that a positive boost to your own attitude is a natural by-product.

Sharon Helps Herself by Helping Her Sister

Sharon asked her sister Casey to meet her for lunch because she needed a lift after learning about their father's illness. Casey didn't much feel like talking with Sharon, but she came over anyhow and made a special effort to be upbeat. When lunch was over, Casey had not only given Sharon a boost, she felt better herself. Both sisters came out ahead.

When you give part of your positive attitude to others, you create a special two-way relationship. The recipient feels better, but so do you. It might seem illogical, but it's true: you actually *keep your positive attitude by giving it away.*

When it comes to giving your positive attitude to others, you can be generous and egocentric at the same time.

What Goes Around Comes Around for Lindsay and Trent

Lindsey is considered a master teacher who freely shares her positive attitude with everyone—students, faculty, and staff. In return, others are constantly reinforcing Lindsey's attitude with compliments and attention, and her students seem to make an extra effort to work hard.

Trent is an outstanding associate—upbeat, respected, productive. He's also a practical joker. Every day he tries to create a little levity to balance the pressure of work. In sharing his good humor he's rewarded by a dedicated staff that works hard to deliver higher productivity because they appreciate the pleasant work environment he promotes.

Opportunities occur daily to give a positive attitude to others—and often a benefit is returned. Taxi drivers who make their passengers laugh will usually increase their tips. Project leaders who give team members well-earned compliments find their team members motivating themselves—resulting in higher productivity, better quality work, and a more successful project. Opportunities abound!

And, it often seems that the results are best when the giving is *toughest*. The less you feel like giving away part of your positive attitude, the more *giving it away* will do for you. Sometimes it can help you get out of a rut.

Julio and Bart Receive by Giving

It was a Day From Hell for Julio. The usual Monday staff meeting dragged on, and he was already behind on the Danvers Project proposal. Just as he was starting to pull it together, Windows melted down, and he had to transfer all the files to his laptop. When he finally left work about 8:00 P.M., all Julio could think of was crashing on the couch to catch the second half of the game. But he'd promised to visit his friend, Lenny, who got out of the hospital over the weekend. The temptation to drive straight home was strong, but he resisted and made his way over to Lenny's. Lenny and his wife really appreciated Julio's visit, and when Julio arrived home he felt refreshed and positive. He caught the highlights on ESPN and fell sound asleep.

Kate had been in a lousy mood for weeks. Last night, discouraged with her present state of mind, she decided to do something nice for her brother, Bart, who was having a difficult time working through a divorce. She called him on the spur of the moment and asked him to go to the beach on Saturday. After a great weekend, Kate returned with a positive outlook. Was it the different environment, the fresh air, or the exercise that caused the change? Yes, yes, and yes—but much of the improvement came from helping Bart to regain his focus, too.

You'll wind up a winner by sharing your positive attitude with others. The attitude giveaway exercise on the next page may help you decide which ways will work best for you.

Attitude Giveaway Exercise

Below are different methods people use to share or pass on a positive attitude. Some approaches may appeal to you; others will not. Review the list, add a few ideas of your own, then pick out three or four approaches that fit your style—three or four ideas that you intend to try at work or in your personal life sometime during the next week. (Make a note of _____.)
today's date

❏ 1. Go out of my way to visit friends who may be having trouble with *their* attitudes.

❏ 2. Be more positive around those with whom I have daily contact.

❏ 3. Transmit my positive attitude to others whenever I use the phone.

❏ 4. Pass on my positive attitude by sending cards or token gifts to someone I care about.

❏ 5. Share my sense of humor by using the flipside technique.

❏ 6. Be more sensitive as a listener so others can regain their positive focus.

❏ 7. Laugh more so my attitude will be noticeable and others will pick it up.

❏ 8. Communicate my attitude through upbeat conversations, by paying compliments to others, etc.

❏ 9. Give my attitude to others by setting a consistent example as a positive person.

❏ 10. _____

❏ 11. _____

❏ 12. _____

Come back to this page in a week or so to note what you tried and how it worked out.

Tried # _____ Results: _____

Tried # _____ Results: _____

Tried # _____ Results: _____

Tried # _____ Results: _____

Adjustment Technique 6:
Look Better to Yourself

Business isn't like Hollywood or Madison Avenue or any other part of our culture where image is *everything*. However, people who think that appearance doesn't count have their heads in the sand.

In the workplace, first impressions do count. Anyone who walks into an office or a work area for the first time takes a *mental snapshot* of its appearance and, consciously or unconsciously, starts to answer the question:

"What kind of work goes on here?"

When you walk past a cubicle, or visit a branch office, or when a new employee joins your department, you take a mental snapshot of the people you see and their surroundings. So, isn't it logical to assume that others who meet you are also taking mental snapshots of you and your work space?

Eventually, these mental snapshots form a picture. It's not a picture you can control, but you can *affect* the appearance you present to others. And, here's the punch line for this topic:

If you *know* that your appearance suggests quality and productivity, it will have a positive effect on your attitude.

We're not talking about looking trendy or being fashion-conscious or about demonstrating that you know all the right people. But, we are talking about *feeling confident* that your appearance signals to others that you do first-rate work. If you develop this feeling of confidence, you will notice its positive impact on your attitude. There is a direct connection between the way you feel about your appearance and a positive attitude.

Several specific things you can do to affect your appearance in ways that suggest quality and productivity are presented on the next two pages. Review the list, think about the possibilities, then put a check mark by any action you think might work for you.

Years ago, Gillette Safety Razor commercials signed off with this slogan: "Look sharp. Feel sharp. Be sharp." It's still good advice today.

 This is not a "glamour" makeover! Everything you do should reflect common sense and fit your work situation. Aim to become reasonably neat and clean for the kind of work you do, appropriate for getting the job done and interacting with others.

ADJUSTING YOUR ATTITUDE BY IMPROVING YOUR APPEARANCE

Here are seven general activities that you can undertake to maintain or improve the way you appear to others. Check (✔) the ideas that you think might work for you. Remember, your goal is to present an image that suggests quality and productivity.

❑ **Look healthy.** Devote time to an exercise program—anything that will create a healthier appearance. Whatever you've been doing, turn it up one notch.

If you've been doing no exercise at all, make it a point to do something every week:

　❑ At work or at the mall, park your car or truck a block away instead of driving around looking for the space closest to the door;

　❑ Walk around the block before you go to bed each night;

　❑ Use the stairs instead of taking the elevator.

If you've been doing some exercise from time to time, but without a regular commitment:

　❑ Choose one specific activity and commit to do it three times a week;

　❑ Sign up for a trial membership at a health club.

If you've been exercising on a regular basis:

　❑ Notch it up to 20 minutes of aerobic activity (plus warm-up and cool-down), three times per week.

If you already do an aerobic workout three times a week:

　❑ Increase your frequency or your miles;

　❑ Maintain your current level and put extra effort into other items on this list.

❑ **Dress a little sharper.** You don't have to spend big money on clothes to improve your appearance. Something new that fits you, fits right, and fits in will usually be okay. If you're uncertain, notice the people who hold the jobs you'd like to have five years from now and take your cue from their personal appearance.

❏ **Pay attention to your face.** The first thing people usually notice about a person is their face, especially their eyes and their smile. So, you can improve your appearance simply by making better eye contact with others and smiling more. Beyond that, "neat and clean" is an adequate minimum standard.

If you have some special feature that affects your attitude—something dental or cosmetic, for example—investigate your out-of-pocket cost for appropriate treatment. Then decide if the benefit is worth the cost—as a one-time expense or as a "gift" to yourself.

❏ **Check your posture.** After your face, one of the next things people notice about you is your posture and the way you carry yourself. Sometimes your posture is a direct indicator of your attitude. You know the feeling: attitude down; shoulders slumped; eyes averted.

❏ Ask your family or close friends how your posture looks.

❏ Go to an electronics superstore where they have demo camcorders set up on the floor. You'll be able to get a view of yourself from various angles. It's a quick, effective way to see yourself and your posture as others see you.

❏ **Take a look at your personal workspace.** Whether you work in a private office or a cubicle, at a work station, on a construction jobsite, or in your car, your personal workspace is part of your appearance. If your workspace isn't reasonably neat and reasonably clean for the kind of work you do, you have an opportunity to "improve your appearance" and your attitude by putting things in reasonable order.

❏ Do the test: when you arrive at work, within five minutes you should be able to find anything you need that's normally kept in your workspace.

❏ If you use a desktop or laptop computer in your work, you should also be able to find any file you might need quickly, even if you have thousands of files. While a messy or disorganized file structure might not be visible to others, you know, and when the mess has you all knotted up you can bet your attitude will crash even if your computer doesn't.

❑ **What about your car or truck?** It's not true that you are what you drive, but the vehicle you drive to work is part of your appearance. You've probably seen at least one car or truck parked next to the dumpster where the only real difference was the size of the wheels.

> ❑ If your car or truck isn't reasonably neat and reasonably clean as compared to other vehicles in the parking lot, then in one afternoon you can "improve your appearance" significantly.

> ❑ If you're a road warrior and the tools of your road life aren't organized and in proper working order, you're not ready to work productively. If something important is missing or broken, you're vulnerable to delays and second-rate presentations; you're not prepared to do effectively what you've been hired to do. Most important, you know if you have deficiencies in these areas, and you'll improve your attitude by doing something about them.

❑ **Be yourself.** Pay attention to what others say, but don't let them make your list or set your priorities. Ignore what you see in the media. Think things through, then stay with your own idea of what your appearance should be. Be different in the way you want to be different. Be comfortable with who you are.

If you feel your personal appearance says "I'm someone you can count on to be organized, be productive, and deliver first-rate work," you can expect to become a more positive person.

Adjustment Technique 7:
Accept the Physical Connection

No one has conclusively proven that there's a clinical relationship between physical well-being and attitude, but even the most cynical researchers in this area concede there is a connection. Please mark your answer to the following questions; the answers are on the next page.

True False

☐ ☐ 1. A 60-minute workout can do as much or more to adjust your attitude as a Happy Hour at the local pub.

☐ ☐ 2. Eating right won't do anything to improve your self-image.

☐ ☐ 3. On a given day, your attitude is likely to be more positive if you feel physically fit.

☐ ☐ 4. A sense of physical well-being can't be stored indefinitely; neither can a positive attitude.

☐ ☐ 5. Regular aerobic exercise will help you stay fit, but it won't affect your attitude.

Everyone seems to be aware of physical fitness, and many people incorporate a workout into their weekly schedule. They talk about their experience and how it demonstrates the "attitude connection."

"My workout does as much for my head as it does for my body."

"Exercise tones up my body and tunes up my outlook."

"I never underestimate what my daily workout can do for me psychologically."

And, many fitness enthusiasts rely on exercise to pull themselves out of an attitudinal rut—to get themselves back on track.

"I've renamed my health club 'The Attitude Adjustment Factory.'"

"When I'm worried or feeling down, I take a long walk. It just pushes negative thoughts right out of my system."

"A tough workout can get me out of a mental rut."

56

But even people who study the practical benefits of superb physical conditioning understand that "getting in shape" is not the goal. No single group in our culture deals more with the psychological aspects of attitude than professional athletes. Increasingly, athletes undertake sophisticated, year-round physical conditioning programs. They realize they must stay in shape to remain competitive. But, if you listen carefully, you'll also hear coaches and managers talk about the link between attitude and physical conditioning.

"We made the playoffs this year because we have a new team attitude."

"I owe my success this season to Coach Lefty. He helped me with the mechanics of my change-up, but more important, he helped me adjust my attitude."

"My success this year is all due to greater self-confidence. I finally began to believe in myself, and when I got my confidence back, my performance improved."

Talent and physical conditioning are essential—but every team has talent and everybody works hard to stay in shape. Most players, coaches, and others who really know the game talk about mental attitude as the one factor that separates champions from winners, and winners from teams who struggle just to make the playoffs.

The similarity to a business in a competitive market is surprising. One high-profit division manager summed up his view this way:

"In our industry, every company has good workers, experienced supervisors, and everybody works hard. We're all in reasonably decent financial shape. We all have about the same kind of equipment and use the same pool of vendors and suppliers. What we have that's unique to our company is the attitude of our people and our ability to work together as a team. It's our edge!"

Answers to the True/False Questions

1. True; both will change your focus, but exercise is better for you and lasts longer; your muscles might he sore the next morning but your head won't hurt.

2. False.

3. True.

4. True.

5. False; regular exercise is an excellent attitude adjuster.

Maintain a Mental/Physical Balance

As you've learned, you can use both mental techniques and physical techniques to adjust your attitude. It's important to keep these two approaches in balance.

The exercise on the next page will help you decide what you plan to do and the balance you want to achieve. Look over everything you've covered so far in Part 2—especially your notes—before you fill out the chart.

Special Note: You may want to do this exercise in pencil or on a photocopy now, then come back and review the chart again after you've finished this book.

Balancing Exercise

In my desire to become a more positive person, I recognize that I need to find a reasonable balance between mental adjustments and physical exercise. This is what I plan to do to achieve that balance. (Be honest!)

Mental I plan to employ these attitude adjustments:	**Physical** My regular exercise program will consist of:
Daily	Daily
Five times a week	Five times a week
Three times a week	Three times a week
Once a week	Once a week
Might as well face it; some things I'm never going to do	Might as well face it; some things I'm never going to do

This page may be photocopied for individual use.

Adjustment Technique 8:
Clarify Your Mission

A person with a clear purpose in life is more likely to have a positive attitude than someone who lacks direction. This purpose doesn't need to be an all-consuming mission—and it can change over time—but it should be strong and clear enough to provide a consistent focus, a sense of priority, and a challenge.

Focusing on "What Counts"

Karen is a Realtor with a steady, consistent track record. She's divorced, and Karen's mission is to make sure her son, age 9, and daughter, age 15, get the best parenting she can possibly provide. She likes her work and takes both children to a weekend open house every spring and fall. College expenses will begin in just a few years, and she's working on her CRP designation because she knows it will help her get more corporate relocation assignments. Her daughter has applied to work at McDonald's next summer.

Carlos started as an apprentice electrician in 1984, became a journeyman in 1988 and a shift foreman in 1995. His mission is to become a senior supervisor, then a manager with his company, a $50+ billion manufacturer with world-wide operations. Carlos works hard, and he's taken two or three supervisory training courses every year for the past seven years.

Beth is office manager for a company that manages 1,200 apartments in a college town. Over the years, she's become the company's computer expert. She's installing a network to connect the office with three branch offices and converting to a new cost accounting system. Her mission is to finish these changes by year-end, while keeping daily operations under control and avoiding a crisis. Beth seems to have a new mission every 18–24 months, and most of them are no easier than her current challenge. She's taking evening classes toward her CPA.

A mission in life provides direction. It helps people maintain a clearer focus, and it seems to dissipate fears and decrease uncertainty. A mission provides a consistent perspective—a base against which to measure or attach new events, opportunities, and challenges. Having direction gives a person a stronger grip on his or her attitude. Negative events and messages seem easier to deal with or control.

Some people seem to shy away from thinking about or clarifying their mission. They say "I don't want anything to control me. I don't need a special challenge. I just want to live day to day." This approach may work for someone who is just starting out—someone with only a few responsibilities. But, it's a very limiting lifetime strategy. People who have no mission and no focus may wonder, at times, why they're not making faster progress and why they're not getting more out of life.

Mission Exercise

Searching for or clarifying a life's purpose can be interesting, challenging, and fun. Here's an exercise to guide you through this process by answering the following question:

What would be your #1 goal–if you had one year to live and you were guaranteed all the resources you needed to be successful?

Answer the question by drawing or sketching a picture, design or symbol that represents your primary purpose. (Carlos might sketch an airplane with him sitting on top of it; Karen might draw a picture of her daughter's college graduation.)

Draw your design inside the circle. Pictures and symbols only, no words.

Whatever you draw represents your primary purpose in life. Think about what you'd need and do to make your mission become a reality.

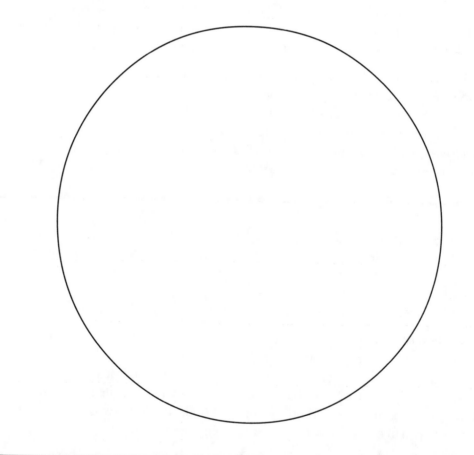

YOUR ACTION PLAN

Take a few minutes and review the eight techniques for adjusting your attitude. Reflect on the answers you've written and the notes you've made in your book.

Although all eight of the attitude adjustment techniques can be used to both maintain and recapture a positive attitude, some may be more effective at any specific time. As you compile your Action Plan, list in the left column things you might do to maintain your attitude and in the right column things you might do to recapture your attitude. Remember, this is your plan; just write down what you think will work for you now. Revise your plan as necessary.

There's also a master copy of this form in the back of this book.

Technique	Maintain	Recapture
Flipside Technique		
Play Your Winners		
Simplify! Simplify!		
Insulate! Insulate!		
Give Your Positive Attitude to Others		
Look Better to Yourself		
Accept the Physical Connection		
Clarify Your Mission		

Key Points from Part 2

The Flipside Technique (page 33)

➤ Look for a humorous angle to diffuse a difficult situation.

➤ Use laughter as a therapeutic treatment.

➤ Humor can jump-start the problem-solving process, but be cautious and sensitive:

– Be aware of the effect of your humor and laughter on others and avoid jokes that might be inappropriate or offensive to someone.

– Don't use humor to laugh at everything and deny the reality of difficult circumstances or problems.

Play Your Winners (page 37)

➤ Everyone deals with both positive factors and messages (winners) and negative factors and messages (losers).

➤ Be alert so losers don't push your winners into the background or make them disappear.

➤ You often have more control over factors (things in your environment) than messages (inputs from others).

➤ Think about your winners.

➤ Talk about your winners.

➤ Reward yourself; enjoy your winners.

Simplify! Simplify! (page 40)

➤ Get rid of unused and unappreciated possessions.

➤ Cut back on commitments and involvements.

➤ Find a better balance between work and your personal life.

➤ Stop putting off the little things.

➤ Let go of worn-out relationships.

Insulate! Insulate! (page 45)

➤ Everyone must learn to live with some "no-win" situations that cannot be easily eliminated, reduced, or avoided.

➤ Work to insulate yourself against negative factors and "no-win" situations.

➤ Phase I Insulators

 – Keep busy.

 – Adopt a "one day at a time" philosophy.

 – Play your winners.

 – Exercise.

 – Use humor.

 – Simplify your life.

 – Concentrate on positive thoughts.

 – Do something for someone else.

 – Spend time with a friend.

➤ Phase II Insulators

 – Talk it out.

 – Work it out.

 – Laugh it out.

 – Pray about it.

 – Change the scene.

➤ Remember: it usually takes some sort of action to accomplish insulation.

➤ Use the Insulation Checklist to develop your own personal approach to insulating your attitude.

Give Your Positive Attitude to Others (page 48)

➤ When you give part of your positive attitude to others, they feel better—and so do you. You keep your positive attitude by giving it away.

➤ The less you feel like giving away part of your positive attitude, the more giving it away will do for you.

➤ Ten ways to give away your positive attitude:

- Go out of your way to visit friends who may be having trouble with their attitudes.

- Be more positive around those with whom you have daily contact.

- Transmit your positive attitude to others whenever you use the telephone.

- Pass on your positive attitude by sending cards or token gifts to people you care about.

- Share your sense of humor by using the flipside technique.

- Be more sensitive as a listener so others can regain their positive focus.

- Laugh more so your attitude will be noticeable and others will pick it up.

- Communicate your attitude through upbeat conversations, by paying compliments to others, etc.

- Give your attitude to others by setting a consistent example as a positive person.

Look Better to Yourself (page 51)

➤ Make sure your appearance suggests quality and productivity.

➤ Look healthy.

➤ Dress a little sharper.

➤ Pay attention to your face.

➤ Check your posture.

➤ Take a look at your personal workspace.

➤ Clean up your car or truck.

➤ Be yourself.

Accept the Physical Connection (page 55)

➤ Whatever amount of exercise you're doing–even if it's zero–turn it up one notch.

➤ Use exercise to pull yourself out of a rut.

➤ Keep a reasonable balance between the mental techniques and the physical techniques you use to adjust your attitude.

Clarify Your Mission (page 59)

➤ Choose a mission that's strong enough to achieve a clear focus, dissipate fears, provide perspective, and decrease uncertainty.

➤ Change your mission as circumstances or your needs change.

Your Action Plan (page 61)

➤ Step 1: Pick out the ideas that can have the most impact on your positive attitude.

➤ Step 2: Write them on your Action Plan.

➤ Step 3: Review the total scope of what you've written to ensure it's doable–then *Just Do It!*

➤ Step 4: See what works and what doesn't.

➤ Step 5: Repeat the ones that work; scrap the ones that don't.

Remember: Your goal is to ensure that your most priceless possession becomes and remains everything *you* want it to be.

Take a Few Minutes to Reflect

You've just finished Part 2 of this book which described eight techniques for adjusting your attitude. Take a short break and go over what you've learned:

➤ Skim through Part 2 and take another look at each of the eight techniques and the notes you made.

➤ As you go over these pages again, write down any new ideas that come to mind.

➤ Review the Key Points covered in Part 2.

➤ Finally, go back and look over your Action Plan; circle two or three items you're going to try out during the next few days.

Now, move on to Part 3 to consider the connection between your attitude and your job.

Attitude

and

Your

Job

Attitude and the Work Environment

Nowhere is your positive attitude more appreciated by others than when you are at work. There are four reasons for this:

➤ Business competition is very demanding; it moves at a fast pace, budgets are tight, and the work itself can sometimes be physically demanding. A positive person makes the work more satisfying and enjoyable for everyone.

➤ Everyone—employees, associates, supervisors—depends upon the positive attitude of others to establish and maintain a team spirit. A positive attitude at all organizational levels and in every location makes everyone's job easier.

➤ Some people have difficult personal lives. Where they work can be a place to find positive attitudes that can help them deal with their difficulties.

➤ Approximately half of a person's waking hours are spent in the workplace. Without some positive attitudes around, this amount of time could seem endless.

Both positive and negative attitudes travel quickly in the workplace. Working near a person with a positive attitude is an energizing experience. He or she can make others feel more upbeat. Working near a negative person is like being trapped in an elevator with a grouchy jerk. Escape is impossible, and the effect of his or her negative attitude is difficult to avoid.

Sam Has It; Max Doesn't

Sam has a little less talent and education than many other associates. But he makes up for his shortcomings with his consistently positive attitude. His supervisor says: "Results? It takes Sam a little longer to get things done, but he's easy to work with and his contribution to the overall productivity of the store is outstanding."

Max is the most dedicated and talented salesman on the floor when working with customers. His personal productivity is high. However, his negative attitude behind the scenes keeps everybody he works with on edge, and his department missed its monthly quota twice last year. Max's negative attitude has made him a "loner" at work.

The Impact is Apparent

A positive work environment often produces fewer mistakes, higher quality, and better productivity. A negative attitude is a distraction. It interferes with everyone's focus, and it consumes time and energy for people to deal with it. The overall attitude in a department, a branch office, on a project, or in a company can be traced to the individual attitudes of each participant.

An observant outsider can tell when a work group is efficient and productive by noticing the attitudes of supervisors and the people who work with and for them. There's more laughter. People are more tolerant of each other. Work is viewed more as a challenge than as a series of demanding, boring tasks. But beware! One negative attitude can turn a harmonious situation sour.

> ➤ A supervisor with a negative attitude puts a damper on every co-worker, and through other supervisors, he or she can spread a negative attitude like a bad cold. Hardly anybody escapes.

> ➤ A small group (clique) with a negative attitude can split a department into opposing camps. Teamwork suffers. Everyone loses.

> ➤ People who work closely together can often overcome a negative attitude from one person in the group. But it takes extra energy and persistence which can distract the group from its goals and undermine its performance.

It's often easy to identify people with positive and negative attitudes when vacations roll around. People with positive attitudes are missed and welcomed back. The absence of those with negative attitudes gives everyone else a much needed vacation.

The point, of course, is that your positive attitude is not only your most precious asset—it's also greatly valued by others.

People motivate themselves. You can give pep talks and talk others into short term bursts of higher productivity, but over the long haul, you can't really motivate someone else. You can just create a climate that encourages or discourages self-motivation. People who have a positive attitude are more likely to motivate themselves to work more efficiently, to be more productive, and to produce better quality. But, they have to do it themselves. And your own positive attitude can make first-rate results possible.

What Do Supervisors Expect?

All you need to do to discover what supervisors appreciate most in team members or people they work with is to check the results from formal appraisals. These six items are included on nearly every appraisal form:

_3_ Works productively

_1_ Has a good attitude

_5_ Turns out first-rate quality

_6_ Has excellent technical skills

_2_ Is dependable

_4_ Makes few mistakes—but owns up to the ones he or she makes and doesn't repeat them

Personnel with (Team Work!)

Look over this list and rank these six items in order of importance. Indicate the priority of your preferences by writing a 1 in your first choice, a 2 in your second choice, and so on until each item has a number.

Most supervisors will rank attitude as a one or a two priority. When asked why, these are the kinds of answers that they give:

"I place attitude near the top of my list because a positive team member not only produces at a high level but makes it easier for others on the team to stay positive and produce more, too."

"Attitude is more important than other performance factors because it leads others to higher levels of accomplishment."

"One person with a negative attitude can turn others negative. On the other hand, somebody who's always positive pulls everyone up and makes my job easier."

Other factors being equal, the person with a positive attitude wins nearly every time. Here's why:

➤ You may not hear it expressed verbally—because it's not something people normally compliment each other on—but your positive attitude is deeply appreciated by everyone you work with.

➤ Through your attitude, you either contribute or subtract from the quality of your work environment. The neutral zone is pretty narrow. Most of the time you're either helping or hurting.

➤ You contribute to productivity through your skills and effort; you also contribute more than you realize by the way your positive attitude plays out through others.

Case Study 3: *Maya & Zora*

Maya and Zora are identical twins; most people can't tell them apart. Both are associates–in different but comparable stores for the same large retail chain; they're equally smart and have received the same amount of training and education. However, Maya is more successful in her career and in her life than Zora.

When the chips are down, Maya is easier to talk to and be around than Zora. Because of this, she is more popular and enjoys her work more. Zora seems to have less personal confidence. She succumbs to negative feelings more than Maya does. Sometimes Maya and Zora talk about this difference between them. Zora often claims that Maya is just lucky and that she isn't. Maya, on the other hand, often claims that Zora just doesn't have as good an image of herself as she should.

On more than one occasion, Maya has said: "Zora, you and I are the same in so many ways, but for some reason you don't see yourself as I see myself. You tear yourself down in your own mind. I build myself up. You have better skills than I do and are more capable than you think you are, but unless you start believing in yourself, things just won't improve for you."

What role has attitude played in the lives of Maya and Zora so far? What might Zora do to help herself? What might Maya do to help her sister?

_____

_____

_____

_____

_____

_____

_____

_____

When you've finished analyzing the case and writing down your ideas and views, see **Comments on the Cases** in the back of this book for important ideas and insights about this case.

A Positive Attitude About Diversity

A major change has taken place in the workforce: the cultural mix of employees has become more diversified. It's not unusual to find several cultures represented in a company, in a branch office, or even within a small work group. People from different ethnic backgrounds, social groups, genders, and lifestyles work to-gether—and depend on each other—to carry out their responsibilities and com-plete projects on time, efficiently, and with first-rate quality.

The performance standards are the same, but the workforce mix is different. A new employee will likely work with and for a wider range of people than those he or she grew up with. People who have been in business for years will likely work with and supervise a wider range of people than those they worked with or supervised in the past.

How Do You Adapt to the New Workforce?

What is your attitude about working with others who are different from you? Ask yourself these ten questions—and answer them **Yes**, **No**, or **Sometimes**:

1. Are you annoyed when someone has trouble with the English language?
   Y (N) S

2. …with someone who stands very close to you when they talk? **(Y) N S**

3. …with a person whose personal lifestyle is very different from yours? **Y (N) S**

4. Is it difficult for you to establish effective working relationships with those who are new to the United States? **Y (N) S**

5. Are you impatient with people who have work habits that are different from your own? **Y (N) S**

6. Do you spend all of your break time and lunch time with people who are just like you? **Y (N) S**

7. Are you a lot slower to accept someone from a different social group? **Y N (S)**

8. Are you uncomfortable with people from cultures that are different from yours? **Y N (S)**

9. Would it damage your attitude if a person of the opposite gender became your supervisor? **Y (N) S**

10. If you had to train a replacement for your position, would you be less enthusiastic about preparing someone a with a very different lifestyle than yours? **Y (N) S**

Few people would say "No" to all ten of these questions. If you answered "No" to more than half of them, it indicates that your attitude will not be affected very much by the diversity of the people you work with. If you responded "Yes" or "Sometimes" to more than half of the questions, it indicates that your attitude might be negatively affected by your feelings about working with people who are different from you. In either case, here are a few useful ideas to think about.

Be Open to Change

The workforce is what it is: more diverse than it used to be. The chances are high that you'll be working with people who are different from you, and *you'll be dependent on each other to achieve common goals.* Your attitude about working together will affect your ability to achieve those goals. And, if you're a supervisor—or want to become one—you'll be more successful if you're able to understand and work effectively with all of the human resources that are available to you.

Be Open-minded

The results from building working relationships with a diverse mix of newcomers can be mutually rewarding.

➤ People from different cultures often bring new ideas, talents, and points of view that broaden the perspective of the "core" group.

➤ People from some cultures seem to have developed characteristics that others might do well to adopt. For example, some ethnic groups seem to be very hard-working and self-motivated; others seem to have an overall positive attitude that is above the norm.

➤ On a personal basis, people from other backgrounds and cultures offer opportunities to learn about their customs, music, and foods. Anyone who builds an effective working relationship with someone different can increase his or her knowledge and open the door to some interesting opportunities.

A Positive Attitude About Diversity

Over the years, Ed has become pretty open-minded about the people he works with. He's a claims supervisor who specializes in handling disaster claims for a large insurance company. "It's a demanding job, and on most situations, we're in and out in 30–60 days. We draw from lots of different labor pools, and I've got to get results from everybody. I don't care about your parents, or your church, or your ponytail. If you can work hard, work smart, and make our policyholders feel good about the way you've handled things, you're okay." Ed's company tracks new business carefully, and they've noted that the company always sees a little surge in new accounts after Ed and "his crew" leave town, and most of it is from referrals.

Anna found it interesting to help train Keiko for her new job with the bank. Later, Keiko invited Anna to her apartment for a home-cooked Japanese dinner and introduced Anna to many Japanese customs. "It was like taking a virtual trip to Japan," said Anna. "I discovered that Japanese people strongly believe in building mutually rewarding relationships."

Elsa is an experienced sales supervisor for a large retailer in the Southeast, and each year she has to staff up for the holiday season—sometimes a dozen or more, all temps. "We get all kinds. They're all pretty good, but every group is different; there's a lot at stake and a lot to learn. Our daily staff meetings are always 30 minutes, not 15 like they used to be. Before I let them go, I go around to each person and make them tell me what I've told them. Not everybody handles English too well, so this is really important. Then I tell them we can be the #1 department if we all work together." It pays—Elsa's been over quota four years straight. "I work extra hard when somebody believes in me," says Gabriella, who is back for the second year.

MAPSON

Cultural diversity in the workforce is here to stay. People who accept the trend with a positive attitude will find it pays off where it counts: in quality, efficiency, and productivity. And, sometimes they'll also find that their positive attitude is an asset that pays an extra dividend: coming to work just "feels better."

Case Study 4: Ramon Wants to Move Up

Ramon is a highly motivated employee with a large hi-tech company. Born in Mexico, he came to America at the age of six, graduated from high school, and is working on his associate degree at the local community college by taking courses at night. At this stage in his career, however, he's having doubts because he's been in his present job for over three years and has been passed over twice when openings for supervisor came up.

Yesterday, Ramon had a long talk with the HRD director. Ramon made the point that he felt he was free of prejudice as far as others were concerned, but that some people in the company might not accept him. He said he had no idea why he's been passed over, and that no one has talked to him about it. They decided they'd work on the problem from both ends. Ramon would talk with his supervisor about the situation, and the HRD director would inquire to see what she could learn.

They met again a week later, and when Ramon asked what the HRD director had discovered, she replied, "The good news, Ramon, is that everybody respects your work record and your productivity. The bad news is that you give the impression that you're kind of negative and unhappy. From what I gathered, when you were passed over for supervisor last year, it was because management feared that you wouldn't set a positive, upbeat pace for your staff. One person said that you often clam up when critical problems are discussed at staff meetings. I think you have a positive attitude somewhere inside you, but you have to start showing it to others."

"But, my work speaks for itself," replied Ramon.

If you were Ramon, how would you go about expressing a more positive attitude even though your natural inclination is to let your work speak for itself?

_____

_____

_____

_____

_____

_____

When you've finished analyzing the case and writing down your ideas and views, see **Comments on the Cases** in the back of this book for important ideas and insights about this case.

A Positive Attitude Affects Career Success

On the job, as in your personal life, your attitude makes a big difference. Building and maintaining healthy, effective relationships in all directions—with people you work for, people you work with, and people who work for you—is a key to success. Unlike golf or tennis, business is a team sport. Nothing contributes more to the process of building effective work relationships than a positive attitude.

Technical Skills Alone Are Not Enough

Good technical skills are essential, but technical skill by itself is not sufficient. Efficiency and productivity are essential, but neither is sufficient by itself. The same holds true for quality and safe practice. In business, results count, but "the way" a person achieves and delivers those results also counts. The most critical and far-reaching aspect of "the way" a person works is his or her attitude. It either helps or hurts that person's efficiency and productivity, and it also helps or hurts the efficiency and productivity of everyone else that person works with—sort of a domino effect.

Barney Wears Out His Welcome

Barney is a car salesman with 20+ years experience. He's always a top producer, his selling skills are superb, and he has a following. But, Barney has worked for fourteen companies since 1981. Despite his extraordinary technical skills, he wears out his welcome quickly and moves on, and often it's not his decision to leave. Patrick, the last manager Barney worked for, sums it up: "Barn can move cars out with the best of them…and he brought some good, new customers in. But, in the 15 months he was here, I probably spent ten percent of my time on 'Barney problems.' His attitude stinks…grumbles all the time…gripes and hollers at everybody. I lost two good salesmen and one person from accounting who just wouldn't put up with it anymore. When we wrapped up the January Sellathon, I sent him on his way. The new guy, Larry, doesn't have Barney's skills, but…you know…the sales crew is a lot more productive. And, Carla from Accounting came back because overall, this is a good place to work."

Individual results contribute to departmental and division results. Division results contribute to company results. But the attitude of each person, department, and project or team must be: achieve results, but also do it in a way that helps others achieve their results. This kind of positive attitude is visible and contributes to the success of anyone who holds it.

Your Attitude and the People You Work For

Of course you know that it's important to be productive, work efficiently, and turn out work that's first-rate quality. It's also important to meet the expectations of the people who you report to. Make sure that your attitude and the goals you set are consistent with the attitude and goals of your manager—plus the person he or she reports to—and the company.

Remember, it's your responsibility to produce results—as an individual or through others. Likewise, it's your manager's responsibility to produce results *through you* and others like yourself. Make sure your attitude shows that you are one of the people your manager can count on to make those results happen.

Your Attitude and the People You Work With

Every activity in business is connected to—and depends on—other activities. Each department is connected to other departments; to others who precede them, follow them, or work side-by-side; to subcontractors and suppliers; and to people and work groups in other time zones. Every activity in business is connected to internal and external *customers.*

Nothing affects these working relationships as much as the attitude of the people who are connected—people who must work together effectively to be successful. No matter what your role or responsibility is, think of yourself as a "crew member" with others like yourself—with your supervisor as the "foreman" of that "crew." Then do your best to make this "crew" as effective as it can be. Through your attitude, do your best to make your "crew" the kind of first-rate group that every other "crew" really wants to work with.

Achieve the results you seek, but do it in a way that helps others achieve the results they seek.

Your Attitude and the People Who Work for You

If you're a leader—or plan to become one—your success depends on getting results *through* the people who work for you. Nothing will affect your relationship with the people you lead more than your consistent—and visible—attitude. If you show up with the Monday Morning Blues, it will affect the attitude of the people you work with. Your positive attitude can set the pace and the tone for everyone.

➤ They'll see more opportunities and be more likely to spot problems in time to avoid major consequences.

➤ They'll look out for each other, and this teamwork will lead to better results.

➤ They'll be more desirable to work with—and the work will be more enjoyable.

Your positive attitude will have a powerful impact on every aspect of their performance—efficiency, productivity, and quality. Their performance is your performance.

Case Study 5: Frank or Hank?

Assume you are the Group VP of a fast-growing, publicly-owned financial services company. You need to select a regional manager for a three-state region that's known to be very competitive. After several interviews, you've narrowed your choice to either Frank or Hank; both are currently branch managers in this region.

Frank is a pro who plays by the rules and usually wins. With a degree in engineering, he goes about everything in a very analytical and methodical manner. For example, he always does thorough research before making a decision. Frank supports other employees, has an excellent record of following through on projects, subscribes to many professional journals, and is on the College of Engineering advisory board at his alma mater. He's supervised three top-performing branches for the company, though none was among the largest or most competitive branches in the region.

Hank is a highly creative and energetic person who is willing to take risks. He takes a more laid-back approach to his job than Frank does. Hank figures that if he takes a positive, light approach to work that good things will happen to both the company and to himself. Everyone likes Hank and works extremely hard for him, but there have been a few loose ends in the branches he's supervised. Still, no one questions his managerial abilities and skills, and he's handled four different branches; two of them were top performers and one of these was one of the most competitive branches in the region.

Who would you select as your regional manager? Why?

_____

_____

_____

_____

How important is attitude as compared to raw intelligence or formal education?

_____

_____

_____

_____

When you've finished analyzing the case and writing down your ideas and views, see **Comments on the Cases** in the back of this book for important ideas and insights about this case.

A Positive Attitude Affects Teamwork

More business successes are won on attitude than technical achievement. A supervisor who knows how to build a positive attitude can lead a departmental workforce with only average experience and skills to achieve high productivity and successful performance. It's called teamwork, and it happens often.

Juanita's Approach

Juanita, a department head for a large state agency, uses three specific techniques to develop positive attitudes with her staff: 1) she always provides encouragement and, when it's earned, she publicly recognizes people; 2) at least once a week, she finds a reason to compliment each employee; 3) she stays positive herself.

Juanita never complains about the skills or experience of her staff. She maintains a sense of humor which makes dealing with a tight budget bearable. Her combination of these three techniques creates a wave of confidence; it's something that other departments notice, and it ripples through the office. Other supervisors sometimes feel Juanita's approach lacks toughness and discipline, but when the ratings are in, her department is always at or near the top.

This is not to imply that she neglects other aspects of supervision. In fact, Juanita covers all the basics. It simply means that attitude is the glue that holds her department together—and turns it into a winner.

All managers, teachers, and volunteer leaders are "coaches." How can you use leadership techniques to achieve consistently high performance? Consider these five ideas.

The Rotten Apple Principle

Given enough time, one rotten apple will spoil the rest of the barrel. Given enough time, one negative staff member will destroy the positive attitude of the others. To prevent such a breakdown, the negative person must be counseled until he or she makes an attitude adjustment—or some other appropriate action is taken. It is essential to protect and maintain the positive attitude of the rest of the staff. Denial and procrastination are not acceptable options; nearly every time, a negative attitude will only fester and get worse.

The Policy of Fair Treatment

Honor the sound principles of fair treatment. Listen to the needs of others, and respect what they say. Treat each person as an individual. Using dehumanizing techniques, like bullying someone or embarrassing them in public, can destroy positive attitudes that have taken months or years to build.

Attitudes Are Caught, Not Taught

The attitudes of followers reflect the attitudes of their leader—especially as these attitudes are expressed in the leader's actions. A leader must "talk the talk," but it's far more important to "walk the walk." And all the talking and walking originate with the leader's own attitude.

The Attitude/Confidence Connection

People with a positive outlook enjoy greater personal confidence. A basketball player without confidence won't make the shot. A sales representative without confidence might as well stay home. A doctor without confidence does every patient a disservice—or worse. A supervisor without confidence will seldom be successful. The foundation for personal confidence is a positive attitude.

The Go-Back Principle

You've probably heard the phrase, "The best thing you can do is get back on the bicycle." This refers to regaining confidence after a fall—or a failure of any kind. The same principle applies to any team situation. Whenever something occurs to undermine, decrease, or destroy someone's positive attitude, immediately start the process of attitude renewal for that person. Don't wait, don't ignore the situation, and especially, don't let the person drift alone. Go back—start the renewal process immediately and give them an opportunity to recapture their positive attitude.

Projecting Your Positive Attitude

It's true that the main focus of this book is the impact your positive attitude has on *you*—how it affects you, how you feel about it, and what you do to maintain and recapture a positive attitude. But, you don't live or work in isolation, and it makes sense to pay some attention to how you project your positive attitude to others. Keep these three questions in mind as you go about your daily business.

How Do You Look?

Take stock of the way you present yourself to others, especially your eyes, your smile, and your posture. Go back and review the key points in *Adjustment Technique 6: **Look Better to Yourself**.* Does your appearance signal that you do first-rate work? Do you look and move like you have a positive attitude?

How Do You Interact with Others?

How well do you listen? Do you pay as much attention to people as to facts and figures? Do you have a reasonable balance between patience and goal-directed urgency? Remember: Your attitude "speaks" so loudly that it overpowers anything and everything you say. If you're lucky, you have some way to get honest feedback from another person about the way you interact with others. Ask—and listen.

How Do You Handle Problems and Difficulties?

It's usually easy to maintain a positive attitude when things are flowing smoothly. But, does your attitude change when problems loom or land on your doorstep? Like it or not, the attitude you project when difficulties appear is the attitude that others remember most clearly. And, it doesn't make much difference whether the problems or difficulties are business or personal—or even if their appearance is your fault or not. To you, your attitude *is what it is*; to others, your attitude *is what they see*. So, it's important to understand how your attitude might change under fire because the attitude you project in tough times will likely be projected instinctively.

A Word of Caution

Don't go overboard by becoming a noisy cheerleader who spends more effort on projecting your attitude than nurturing it. And above all, don't try to display what you don't possess. If your attitude isn't what you want it to be, resist the temptation to project an edited version. Pull back some, use the techniques you learned about in Part 2, recapture a positive attitude—then project the real thing.

Key Points from Part 3

Attitude and the Work Environment (page 69)

➤ A positive person makes the work more satisfying and enjoyable for everyone.

➤ Supervisors depend upon the positive attitudes of others to establish and maintain a team spirit that is focused on efficiency, productivity, and quality. Positive attitudes at all organizational levels, and at every business location, make everyone's job easier.

➤ Some people have difficult personal lives. Where they work can be a place to find positive attitudes that can help them deal with their difficulties.

➤ Many people have a mission that they pursue through their work performance, and the presence of positive attitudes affects their ability to accomplish that mission.

➤ One negative attitude can affect everyone in the group.

  – A supervisor with a negative attitude puts a damper on every co-worker, and through other supervisors, he or she can affect an entire office, store, project, or company.

  – A small group (clique) of negative workers can split a department, office, or work group into opposing camps, and everyone loses.

  – People who work closely together can often overcome a negative attitude from one person in the group. But it takes positive attitudes all around—and it takes extra work and often cuts into performance.

➤ Most supervisors value—and expect—a positive attitude from the people they work with.

A Positive Attitude About Diversity (page 73)

➤ In business, you'll be working with people who are different from you, and *you'll be dependent on each other to achieve common goals.* Your attitude about working together will affect your ability to achieve those goals.

➤ If you're a supervisor—or want to become one—you'll be more successful if you are able to understand and work effectively with all of the labor resources that are available to you.

➤ People from different cultures often bring new ideas, talents, and points of view that broaden the perspective of the "core" group.

➤ People from some cultures seem to have developed characteristics that others might do well to adopt—for example, attitudes toward hard work, self-motivation, an overall positive attitude that is above the norm.

➤ On a personal basis, people from other backgrounds and cultures offer opportunities to learn about their customs, music, foods, and other interesting opportunities.

A Positive Attitude Affects Career Success (page 77)

➤ Technical skills alone are not enough.

➤ Make sure your attitude shows that you are one of the people your supervisor can count on to make results happen.

➤ No matter what your role or responsibility is, think of yourself as a "crew member" with others like yourself—with your supervisor as the "foreman" of that "crew." Then do your best to make this "crew" as effective as it can be.

➤ As a supervisor, your positive attitude will have a powerful effect on every aspect of the performance of the people who work for you—their efficiency, their productivity, and the quality of the work they deliver.

 – Ensure that everyone on your staff is on the same page—efficiently focused on the goals in the company's business plan.

– Achieve productivity by basing your actions on a positive attitude that includes: encouragement and teamwork; active, two-way communication; a continuous search for better ways to do the work; and respect for the technical skills and problem-solving skills of the people you supervise.

– Stay upbeat, focus on quality, and never overlook defective work.

A Positive Attitude Affects Teamwork (page 81)

➤ One negative person in a crew or department can destroy the positive attitude of others.

➤ Listen to the needs of others, respect what they say, and treat each person as an individual.

➤ Attitudes are caught, not taught. Your attitude "speaks" so loudly, it overpowers anything you say.

➤ The foundation for personal confidence is a positive attitude.

➤ Immediately start the attitude renewal process whenever something occurs to undermine, decrease, or destroy someone's positive attitude.

Projecting Your Positive Attitude (page 83)

➤ You don't live or work in isolation, and it makes sense to pay some attention to how you project your positive attitude to others.

➤ How do you look? Check your eyes, smile, and posture to ensure they signal that you do first-rate work.

➤ How do you interact with others? Do you really listen? Do you pay attention to people? Find a way to get honest feedback from another person, and listen to it.

➤ The attitude you project when problems or difficulties appear is the attitude that others remember most clearly. Understand how your attitude might change under fire.

➤ If your attitude isn't what you want it to be, pull back some, use the techniques you learned about in Part 2, recapture a positive attitude–and then project it.

"Listening isn't a skill, it's a discipline. All you have to do is shut up."

– Peter Drucker

Protecting Your Most Priceless Possession

Protecting Your #1 Asset

What if you and fifty people you work with each made up a list of your current problems, put the sheets in a box and mixed them up, then each drew a sheet (not your own) from the box…

What would you learn?

Of course, everybody would end up with a list of problems. Some people would discover their own problems are fewer and less serious than those on the list they drew. This would probably help their attitude. Others would discover that their problems are more severe, but they might also realize that nobody is problem-free. If taken one step further, the experiment would reveal something else even more significant and surprising: some people with severe problems would be among those with a positive attitude.

What does this mean?

It says that the number and severity of problems—money problems, relationship problems, health problems, work problems, emotional problems—does not determine a person's attitude. This means *you have the capacity to hold a positive attitude in all kinds of circumstances.*

This is true, even when a new, major problem disrupts your life. It's the *way* you deal with the problem—including your *attitude*—that is decisive. Following are some ideas for dealing with two common situations.

Be a Problem-Solver

Step 1: Slow Down, Gain a Better Perspective

Whenever a heavy problem hits, it's a good idea to back away some—to gain the best possible focus. This is sometimes difficult to do, and people use various techniques: walk around the block, "sleep on the problem," take a mini-vacation, seek the advice of another person. Such actions can produce a more objective understanding of the situation: it's easier to sort out the real issues and it's easier to generate a creative list of possible solutions. And, occasionally the size of a problem will seem to decrease when you slow down, take a break, and view it again.

Step 2: Think the Problem Through in a Logical Way

Problem solving is a logical process. First, get all the facts and sort out the real issue from its symptoms. The real issue usually stands out from its symptoms this way: if you *added* or *changed* or *removed* this one factor, the problem would be solved. Often a symptom will stand out, but even if you add, change, or remove this one factor, the problem will remain. It's only a symptom, and you must continue your search for the real issue.

Next, come up with a list of possible solutions. Be creative, and don't try to "jump to the answer" right away. Then analyze each solution carefully to pick the best one. Then, of course, *do it*—and check to see if treating the one factor you identified actually solved the problem. If it has, you're finished; if it hasn't, start again at the top.

Step 3: Live with the Solution Gracefully

Sometimes the best solution isn't 100% ideal. But once you make a decision, give it your best effort. This usually means recapturing your previous attitude so you don't continue to revisit the problem over and over in your mind.

Be Aware of Major Lifestyle Changes

Few events can test a positive attitude more than making the adjustment to a new lifestyle. Moving to a new part of the country, making a career change, adjusting to a big promotion, coping with a job cutback, or going through the transition of a break-up, a divorce, or retirement can pull your attitude through a knothole. If you're dealing with a major lifestyle change, consider these three suggestions.

View the Change as an Opportunity

Remember the *High Expectancy Success Theory*: the more you expect out of a new situation the more you are likely to find. If you can approach a lifestyle transition with a positive attitude, the battle is half won before you start. Most transitions are a mixture of difficult and rewarding factors, and if you can sustain your positive focus, you'll find that your view of the events you experience and the messages you receive will be more positive. The *momentum* of your attitude will be positive.

Expect that Attitude Adjustments Will Be Necessary

Anticipate the need for periodic attitude adjustments, and get started sooner rather than later by taking advantage of the eight adjustment techniques presented in Part 2. Be honest with yourself, understand that your attitude is going to take a hit, and do something about it. People who just allow a difficult transition to unfold without taking any action usually wake up later to discover that their positive attitude has turned negative—and this can turn a difficult transition into a trauma.

Realize that Temporary Letdowns Are Normal

Downers are normal and don't often reach the "depression stage" where professional help is required. You'll have to pay attention to your own progress, though. Setbacks can occur after some progress has been made, but before the transition is complete. If you sense a feeling of temporary letdown, review the eight techniques, and take action to turn your attitude back in a positive direction.

Key Points from Part 4

Be a Problem-Solver (page 90)

➤ Slow down until you gain a positive perspective.

➤ Think the problem through in a logical way.

➤ Live with the solution gracefully.

Be Aware of Major Lifestyle Changes (page 91)

➤ View the change as an opportunity.

➤ Accept the fact that some refocusing will be necessary.

➤ Recognize that temporary letdowns are normal.

➤ Never give up.

Your Attitude Is Your Most Priceless Possession

A wise person once said, "If you place more emphasis on keeping a positive attitude than on making money, you'll be successful and the money will take care of itself." Pursuit of wealth and attitude have little to do with each other; the rich don't automatically enjoy a positive attitude—in fact, many wealthy people are miserable while many people with fewer resources are happy and at peace with themselves. A positive attitude is acquired through work and practice, and it's available to everyone.

Each person is free to select his or her most important personal possession. Some choose money or other worldly things; others place their highest value on personal relationships. Only a few think of their personal attitude as a "possession," but it's worth considering because so many good things start with a positive attitude.

A positive attitude can help you enhance your career (money), create better personal relationships (happiness), and come closer to reaching your life goals (success—as *you* define it). You win in all directions.

That's why *a positive attitude is your most priceless possession!*

YOUR ACTION PLAN

Technique	Maintain	Recapture
Flipside Technique		
Play Your Winners		
Simplify! Simplify!		
Insulate! Insulate!		
Give Your Positive Attitude to Others		
Look Better to Yourself		
Accept the Physical Connection		
Clarify Your Mission		

ACTION IDEAS

From Page #	Check here when you transfer an idea to your "To Do" List ➤	

Comments on the Cases

Case 1: Maria's Mood Swings (page 22)

First, realize that it's difficult to help others control their attitudes. But, you can make suggestions when someone appears to be receptive, and you can make these suggestions in a positive, sensitive way. Here's what you might say to Maria:

➤ "You're on overload. If you could just trim back some on the energy you pour into all your responsibilities, maybe you could cut away some time for yourself and be able to relax more."

➤ "Try to lighten up—laugh a little more."

➤ "You're really doing okay—a lot better than most of the rest of us. But, the little things seem to hit you harder—even though these little things always seem to disappear quickly. When your kids get sick, they bounce back in a couple of days. And, last year you pretty much caught up on your holiday bills in a month or so. Try to see past the little things and think about all the positive stuff that's going on."

Case 2: Rita vs. Dawn (page 27)

Rita is steady, open, responsive, and dependable—sort of the strong, silent type. She gets results and most of her effect on the attitude of her staff flows from the work itself—if productivity is running high, everyone feels okay. Rita doesn't take many actions that are intended solely to improve the attitude of her staff, and if performance takes a dip, her approach might slow down or delay a turnaround. Rita would really benefit from the techniques presented in Part 2 of this book.

Not a day goes by without Dawn doing something to keep the attitude of her staff healthy. Her positive attitude is obvious, and she repeatedly "gives it away" to others. She's active, and her positive effect on the attitude of her staff shows up in the effort they consistently put out. But, Dawn sometimes undermines all this by skipping over some of the basics of good supervision, especially planning and attention to detail, and productivity takes a hit.

Dawn's temperament is probably better suited to a fast-growing company, but she must pay attention to the basics or she won't last long. Rita's temperament is probably better suited to a stable company, but she must take steps to retain or recapture a positive attitude when things turn down.

Case 3: Maya & Zora (page 72)

Somewhere along the way, Maya learned to take a more positive view of herself than Zora did. Maya's more positive self-image enabled her to see everything in a more positive light. This attitude of self-confidence has helped Maya make more of her career and life so far. But it's not too late for Zora to build a more positive self-image and gain greater self-confidence. Three of the techniques in Part 2 would be especially helpful to Zora: Play Your Winners, Insulate! Insulate! and Clarify Your Mission.

Case 4: Ramon Wants to Move Up (page 76)

Ramon needs to be a little less intense on the job. He's not communicating in an open, relaxed manner with his staff or with other supervisors. In his effort to be accepted by others, he may be overcompensating on the technical side of his job and neglecting to build strong, open relationships. Ramon may have a positive attitude "somewhere inside," but unless he brings it out in the open, others will continue to see his attitude as negative. If Ramon wants to move up, he'll need to open up, especially when problems are discussed at staff meetings. He should make a copy of page 74, *Projecting Your Positive Attitude*, and tape it to his bathroom mirror.

Case 5: Frank or Hank? (page 80)

The complexity of this assignment is not technical—it lies in the competitive pressures in the region. Cooperation, communication, and enthusiasm will probably have more impact on success than problem-solving skills. It will be essential to maintain a positive attitude in all branches and among all branch managers to move this region to the top.

For regional manager, Hank has the edge. Even if a tough technical problem comes up, the kind of positive attitude he promotes is a better "problem-solving resource" than the technical skills Frank offers.

Where teamwork is involved, a positive attitude will usually win out over raw intelligence or an extensive formal education.

Glossary

Attitude: a person's general disposition or mood; a mental "starting point" for viewing life and the people and events in it.

Charisma: a special leadership quality that captures the imagination of others and inspires commitment to a person, cause, or goal.

Clutter Areas: minor negative factors, entanglements, obligations, possessions, commitments, and other complications that make it difficult for a person to remain positive.

Diversity: a cultural mix of employees that includes people from different ethnic backgrounds, social groups, genders, and lifestyles.

Environmental Shock Waves: attitudinal tremors caused by external forces and events such as financial tensions, personal disappointments, family problems, and health concerns.

High Expectancy Success Theory: the more one expects from a situation, the more success one will achieve.

Insulators: techniques for minimizing the effect of negative factors by isolating them or becoming detached from them.

Negative Drift: a gradual drift toward a negative attitude that sometimes occurs even when everything is going smoothly.

Perception: the process of viewing and interpreting the world using the senses— sight, hearing, taste, touch, and smell.

Personality: the unique mix of physical and mental traits found in a person.

Self-image: one's view of one's own abilities, traits, potential, and worth.

Serendipity: the tendency to make valuable or positive discoveries by accident.

Additional Reading

Braham, Barbara. *Finding Your Purpose.* Crisp Series, 2003.

Braham, Barbara and Christine Wahl. *Be Your Own Coach.* Crisp Series, 2000.

Carlson, Richard. *Don't Sweat the Small Stuff.* NY: Hyperion, 1999.

Chapman, Elwood. *Life Is an Attitude.* Crisp Series, 1992.

Chapman, Elwood and Wil McKnight. *The New Supervisor,* Crisp Series, 2002.

Godin, Seth. *Wisdom, Inc.* NY: HarperBusiness, 1995.

Hill, Napoleon. *Think and Grow Rich.* North Hollywood, CA: Wilshire Book Co., 1999.

Hill, Norman. *Improving Peer Relationships.* Crisp Series, 1996.

Lloyd, Sam R. *Developing Positive Assertiveness.* Crisp Series, 2002.

Lloyd, Sam R. and Tina Berthelot. *Self-Empowerment.* Crisp Series, 2002.

Ornish, Dean. *Love & Survival.* NY: HarperCollins, 1999.

Palladino, Connie. *Developing Self-Esteem.* Crisp Series, 1994.

Peale, Norman Vincent. *The Power of Positive Thinking.* NY: Ballantine, 1996.

Peters, Tom. *The Brand You 50.* NY: Alfred A. Knopf, 1999

Raber, Merrill, George Dyck, and Barbara Preheim. *Stress Management.* Crisp Series, 2005.

Scott, Dru. *Stress That Motivates.* Crisp Series, 2002.

Simons, George. *Working Together.* Crisp Series, 2002.

St. James, Elaine. *Simplify Your Life.* NY: Hyperion, 1994.

von Oech, Roger. *A Kick in the Seat of the Pants.* NY: HarperCollins, 1986.

von Oech, Roger. *A Whack On the Side of the Head.* NY: Warner Books, 1998.

Also Available

Books•Videos•Computer-Based Training Products

If you enjoyed this book, we have great news for you. There are over 200 books available in the *Crisp Fifty-Minute*™ *Series*. For more information visit us online at
www.axzopress.com

Subject Areas Include:

Management
Human Resources
Communication Skills
Personal Development
Sales/Marketing
Finance
Coaching and Mentoring
Customer Service/Quality
Small Business and Entrepreneurship
Training
Life Planning
Writing

VERQ